PC-DOS & MS-DOS

A READY REFERENCE MANUAL

CRAIG A. WOOD

Stephen F. Austin State University
Nacogdoches, Texas

The Benjamin/Cummings Publishing Company, Inc.

Redwood City, California • Fort Collins, Colorado
Menlo Park, California • Reading, Massachusetts • New York
Don Mills, Ontario • Wokingham, U.K. • Amsterdam • Bonn
Sydney • Singapore • Tokyo • Madrid • San Juan

Dedicated

To my wife Ellen and sons Deron and Ryan for their constant love, patience, and understanding during the preparation of this book.

To my parents, Nelson and Lousie Wood, for their life of love and support and for their encouragement of my desire to become a teacher.

This book was produced by Benjamin/Cumming's in–house composition system.

Library of Congress Cataloging-in--Publication Data

Wood, Craig A.
PC–DOS & MS–DOS: a ready reference manual/by Craig A. Wood
p. cm.
Bibliography: p.
Includes index.
ISBN 0–201–16730–5
1. PC DOS (Computer operating system) 2. MS–DOS (Computer operating system) I. Title. II. Title: PC–DOS and MS–DOS.
QA76.76.063W657 1987 87–25382
005.4'46--dc19 CIP

The procedures and applications presented in this book have been included for their instructional value. They have been tested with care, but are not guaranteed for any particular purpose. The publisher does not offer any warranties or representations, nor does it accept liabilities with respect to the programs or applications.

Reprinted with corrections September, 1989

ISBN 0–201–16370–5

13 14 15 16 17 18 19 20 AL 95949392

Preface

WHY PURCHASE THIS BOOK?

Because this book will assist you in learning DOS for use on your personal computer, and after you have mastered the basic concepts of DOS, it will provide you with a quick reference guide to DOS commands and procedures.

This Ready Reference Manual will help you become a more effective personal computer user. It provides you with a summary of commonly used DOS commands and procedures. It is designed to assist you in performing DOS tasks such as preparing disks, viewing information on disks, and manipulating files of information.

Unlike most DOS books, the material in this book is organized by function rather than by command. This organization allows you to locate a particular task you want to perform without first knowing the DOS commands associated with the task.

This book provides in-depth coverage of the DOS commands and concepts that are necessary to effectively utilize a fixed (hard) disk. In addition, Appendix B consists of an abbreviated reference manual for the IBM PC-DOS commands through DOS Version 3.30. The command format and a brief description are given for each DOS command.

EQUIPMENT UTILIZED

The material presented in this book covers all versions of IBM PC-DOS and MS-DOS. While the research for this book was done on a variety of personal computers, including IBM, Texas Instruments, Compaq, and Zenith personal computers, the procedures outlined in this book were performed on an IBM PC AT using IBM PC-DOS Version 3.20. The IBM PC AT contained one megabyte of memory, a 1.2MB diskette drive (drive A), a 360KB diskette drive (drive B), and a 30MB fixed disk drive (drive C). PC-DOS and MS-DOS Versions 2.10, 2.13, 3.20, and 3.30 were utilized in the development of the material in Appendix B.

The following books are suggested for further reading about DOS: *PC-DOS: Introduction to High-Performance Computing* by Peter Norton, *Running MS-DOS* by Van Wolverton, and *DOS: The Complete Reference by Kris James.*

ACKNOWLEDGMENTS

Many people participated in the development of this book. I thank the following individuals, who reviewed the manuscript and provided helpful comments and suggestions: Warren J. Boe, University of Iowa; Catherine Garrison, The Softwerks; Robert M. Goldhamer, National Education Corporation; Fred C. Homeyer, Angelo State University; Deborah R. Lafferty; and Arthur A. Strunk. I thank Orlynn R. Evans and Richard L. Robertson, computer science faculty members at Stephen F. Austin State University, for sharing ideas with me about some of the topics in this book. I also thank Karen E. Leath for her assistance in the manuscript preparation using a word processor and for her comments and suggestions resulting from her review of the manuscript.

A special note of thanks goes to Sharon A. Williams for her assistance and comments in the development of the book outline and for her assistance in the preparation of some initial material for the book.

Special thanks also go to Keith Wollman, my sponsoring editor at Addison-Wesley, who first believed that there was a need for this material and then provided me with valuable support and direction during the writing of this book. Thanks, Keith.

Craig A. Wood
Nacogdoches, Texas

Contents

1 Introduction to DOS

The material in this chapter will introduce you to some important DOS concepts and to some computer terminology. This information is intended to give you a quick overview of DOS, disk drives, and disk files. Most of the topics presented here are covered in more detail later in the book.

WHAT IS DOS?

DOS is a collection of special programs that supervise and control the operation of your personal computer. These programs allow you to create and manage files, execute programs, and use different devices, such as a printer, that may be attached to your personal computer. The term DOS is an acronym for **Disk Operating System**. DOS for the IBM Personal Computer family is commonly referred to as **PC-DOS**. DOS was originally developed for IBM by Microsoft Corporation, a leading company in software for personal computers. Microsoft also provides versions of DOS for many other types of personal computers. These versions of DOS are commonly referred to as **MS-DOS (Microsoft DOS)**. There are only minor differences between comparable versions of PC-DOS and MS-DOS. Consequently, only the term DOS will be used in this book.

When you purchase DOS for or with a personal computer, you should get a comprehensive disk operating system manual, a DOS System diskette, and a DOS Supplemental Programs diskette. The names on the diskette labels may vary with different versions of DOS.

WHAT ARE DOS COMMANDS?

Each of the special programs that is included in DOS has a unique name assigned to it. A **DOS command** is a character string specification that references the name of a DOS program. That is, DOS commands specify the execution of DOS programs. You may say that a certain DOS command performs a particular task, but remember that this statement has the following meaning: The DOS command dictates the execution of the appropriate DOS program that performs the assigned task.

Each version of DOS has a certain set of programs that are identified with DOS commands. Sometimes the terms DOS commands and DOS programs are used interchangeably. Appendix B contains a complete list of the DOS commands through DOS Version 3.30.

PARTS OF DOS

DOS programs can be divided into the following four logical categories: DOS system files (programs), internal DOS commands (programs), external DOS commands (programs), and DOS utility programs. Depending upon the context of a statement, the term DOS can be used to include all or part of these categories. Normally, the term DOS is used to refer to the DOS system files.

DOS System Files

The term **DOS system files** is used to denote three files, two hidden system files and the visible system file COMMAND.COM. In PC-DOS the **hidden files** are called IBMBIO.COM and IBMDOS.COM. (In MS-DOS they are usually called IO.SYS and MSDOS.SYS.) All input information (such as input from a keyboard, a mouse, or a communications card) and all output information (such as output to a display screen, a disk, or a printer) are handled (processed) by the programs contained in the two hidden files.

The **IBMBIO.COM** (Basic Input Output) program handles the input and output between the computer and its peripheral devices such as a disk or a printer.

The **IBMDOS.COM** program forms the heart of DOS. It receives all requests for DOS service functions and converts them into a form to send to IBMBIO.COM.

The **COMMAND.COM** program is called the **DOS command processor** and is the interface between you and DOS. COMMAND.COM displays the system prompt, accepts commands from the keyboard, and interprets the commands so that they can be acted upon by DOS.

Your personal computer is considered to be at **command level** if all three DOS system programs are resident in your computer's memory and a DOS system prompt is displayed on your screen.

Internal DOS Commands

DOS commands (programs) that reside in memory as part of DOS are called **internal DOS commands**. The command processor COMMAND.COM contains the programs that are associated with each of the internal DOS commands.

External DOS Commands

DOS commands (programs) that are contained on disks as program files are called **external DOS commands**. These files have the extension .COM or .EXE as part of their name. When an external DOS command is used, the command processor COMMAND.COM loads the appropriate program file from disk into memory and then initiates its execution.

DOS Utility Programs

Several programs that come on the DOS diskettes are not considered to be DOS commands. These special programs are called **DOS utility programs**. They may be helpful in editing files, linking programs together, or performing other specialized tasks.

Batch Commands

DOS allows you to build a file of DOS commands and then execute these commands as a group. Such a file is called a **batch file** and has the extension .BAT as part of its name. When a batch file name is used as a command, it is referred to as a **batch command**.

DOS Diskettes

One of the diskettes that comes in the DOS package usually contains the three DOS system files, the external DOS command files, and a line editor program. This diskette is referred to as the **DOS System diskette** or the **DOS diskette**. A second diskette usually contains several DOS utility programs and a variety of BASIC language programs. This diskette is referred to as the **DOS Supplemental Programs diskette** or the **DOS Supplemental diskette**.

DIFFERENT VERSIONS OF DOS

DOS has been revised several times since the introduction of the first version of DOS, Version 1.00. The **DOS version number** is displayed in the format **X.xx**, where X denotes a major revision number and xx denotes a minor revision number. DOS is revised to add more capability, to take advantage of advances in computer equipment, and to correct errors. A change in xx, the number following the decimal point, indicates a minor change that leaves DOS virtually the same. A change from DOS Version 3.10 to Version 3.20 is an example of such a change. A change in X, the number preceding the decimal point, indicates a major change in

DOS. A change from Version 2.10 to 3.10 is an example of a major change in DOS.

WARNING: Since all parts of DOS work very closely together, you should be careful not to mix parts of DOS from two different versions. Unpredictable things can happen from mixing different versions of DOS, such as losing an entire data disk.

DISK DRIVES

A personal computer normally contains at least one and maybe two diskette drives. The specifications **A:** and **B:** are used to denote the diskette drives. If a personal computer contains a **fixed disk (hard disk) drive**, the specification **C:** is used to denote it. The term **disk (disk drive)** is used to specify both a diskette (diskette drive) and a fixed disk (fixed disk drive).

Diskette and fixed disk drives are characterized by the number of characters that they can store on a disk. The term **byte** is used to denote one character of information. The letter **K** is an abbreviation for kilo, which means one thousand. A **360KB diskette drive** can store approximately 360,000 bytes of information on a **360KB diskette** and is commonly referred to as a **double-sided double-density diskette drive**. The letter **M** is an abbreviation for mega, which means one million. A **1.2MB diskette drive** can store approximately 1,200,000 bytes of information on a **1.2MB diskette** and is commonly referred to as a **high-density diskette drive.** Care must be taken to use the proper diskettes in the appropriate diskette drives. A 30MB fixed disk drive can store approximately 30,000,000 bytes of information on the fixed disk.

Note: Sometimes K is used to denote the value of 2^{10}, which is 1024. Sometimes M is used to denote the value of 2^{20}, which is 1,048,576.

If a computer system is at command level, the **normal DOS prompt** consists of a disk drive letter followed by the "greater than" character (>). The **default disk drive** or **default drive** is specified by the drive letter appearing in the normal DOS prompt. For example, the DOS prompt A> implies that the system is at command level and diskette drive A is the default disk drive.

ENTERING DOS COMMANDS

The instructions that you give DOS are called **commands.** In order for you **to enter a DOS command** the following steps must be performed. First, your system must be at command level. Second, you must press the keys on your keyboard that generate a command name and its parameters using proper syntax (punctuation and grammar). This sequence of characters is called a **command line**. For example, a typical command line may look like

```
DISKCOPY A: B:
```

where DISKCOPY is a command name and A: and B: are parameters. Third, you must press the **Enter (Return)** key to end the command and send the command line to the DOS command processor for appropriate processing.

If you enter an invalid command, a command with improper syntax, or a command that DOS cannot locate in memory or on a disk, then DOS displays the following message: *Bad command or file name.* DOS makes no distinction between uppercase and lowercase alphabetical characters in a DOS command.

In this book, each time you are asked to enter a DOS command, you should assume that your personal computer is at command level with the DOS prompt being displayed. Consequently, **to enter a DOS command**, you only enter the command sequence following the DOS prompt. Several DOS commands ask you to respond to a question by displaying (Y/N). With some of these commands, pressing the Y or N key constitutes a valid response. In other commands you must press the Y or N key and then the Enter key to have a valid response. The statement "enter Y" or "enter N" will be used to denote either of the above responses.

Using the correct syntax to enter a DOS command involves the proper use of delimiters. A **delimiter** is a special character, such as a space, comma (,), or slash (/), that is used to separate items in a list or sequence. In general, spaces are used as delimiters in DOS command lines; that is, spaces are used to separate a DOS command name from its parameter list and to separate individual parameter fields. Spaces are required between the different parts of a DOS command line that do not already contain delimiters. If a delimiter is already present, a space may also be included before the delimiter to make the command line more readable. The formal syntax structure showing where spaces are required for each DOS command is given in Appendix B.

DISK FILES AND NAMING

Information on a disk is organized into files. In particular, a **disk file** or **file** is a collection of related information that is treated as a basic unit of storage. In order for DOS to identify a file on a disk, files must be assigned names.

Naming a Disk File

The name of a disk file is referred to as a **file name** and consists of two parts. The first part of a file name is denoted by **filename** and consists of at least one and up to eight of the following characters:

```
A-Z a-z 0-9 $ & # @ ! % - _ ` ( ) { }
```

Some versions of DOS may allow the use of additional special characters in a file name. The second part of a file name is called the **extension of the filename, filename extension, file extension**, or just **extension**. It consists of a period followed by one to three valid filename characters. The notation **.ext** is normally used to denote a filename extension. Filename extensions are an optional part of file names. The notation **filename[.ext]** is used to specify a file name where **[.ext]** denotes that the extension is optional.

A file name may be preceded by a disk drive designator (A:, B:, or C:) and/or information about where to locate the file on a disk. The term **file specification** is used to denote a sequence of characters that completely identifies a file and where to find it.

File Naming Conventions

A file name should give you a general idea of what information is in the file. Proper naming of files can save you a great deal of time when searching for a particular file. You should note that DOS does not make a distinction between uppercase and lowercase alphabetical characters in a file name.

Wildcard (Global) File Name Characters

DOS allows you to specify groups of file names through the use of two special characters. The characters ***** and **?** are called **wildcard (global) file name characters** when they are used in a file name. The asterisk (*) can be used to represent zero or more characters at the end of a filename or filename extension, while the question mark (?) can be used to represent a single character in a filename or filename extension.

USER (VISIBLE) FILES AND HIDDEN FILES

Disk files can be separated into the following two categories: user (visible) files and hidden files. A **user** or **visible file** is a file that you as a user can access through normal DOS commands. File names for user files are listed on the screen when DOS displays information about files on a disk. A **hidden file** is a file that you as a user cannot access through normal DOS commands. File names for hidden files are not listed when DOS displays information about files on a disk.

Types of User (Visible) Files

The type of a user file is normally dictated by the format of the information in the file. Three special file formats (text, COM, and EXE) and two general file formats (language and application) are presented in this section.

Text files are data files that contain **alphanumeric** (both alphabetic and numeric) and special symbol characters in an ASCII format. **ASCII** is an acronym for American Standard Code for Information Interchange and refers to a code scheme that computers use to represent characters of information. Text files are sometimes referred to as **ASCII files** or **ASCII format files.**

COM files contain executable (binary, machine language) programs that can be loaded directly into memory and executed without any modifications being made to the programs. The name COM file comes from the .COM filename extension.

EXE files contain executable programs that need to be loaded into memory with some address modifications being made before they can be executed. The name EXE file comes from the .EXE filename extension.

Files containing programs written in a programming language such as BASIC are called **programming language files**. These files contain information that a corresponding language processor can read and translate into executable programs. BASIC language files have .BAS as a filename extension.

Application programs create **application data files** in a format that can be read and understood by that application. Application data files have filename extensions associated with the application. For example, a word processing application might use .DOC as a filename extension, and a spreadsheet (worksheet) application might use .WKS as a filename extension.

DOS DEVICE NAMES

DOS has special names called **DOS device names** assigned to input/output (**I/O**) devices such as the keyboard, the display screen, and the printer. These device names have a special meaning when used in a DOS command and are reserved for use only with the assigned devices.

CON is an abbreviation for console. CON is assigned to the keyboard for input and the display screen for output.

PRN is an abbreviation for printer. It is an output device and refers to the parallel printer that DOS uses unless you instruct DOS otherwise. **LPT1** is another abbreviation for printer and is equivalent to PRN.

USE OF ITALIC CHARACTERS FOR DOS MESSAGES

Italic characters are used in Chapters 2 through 9 of this book to denote the information that DOS commands display on the screen. This information includes the DOS prompt, DOS messages, and output from DOS commands. Since the procedures outlined in Chapters 2 through 9 were performed on an IBM PC AT using IBM PC-DOS Version 3.20, the wording and timing of DOS messages and output from DOS commands in these chapters may vary with different personal computers and different versions of DOS.

2 Starting (Booting) DOS

The material in this chapter shows you how to start DOS running in your personal computer and how to make backup copies of the DOS diskettes using the external DOS command DISKCOPY. Four internal DOS commands—DATE, TIME, CLS, and VER—are also presented in this chapter.

BOOTING THE SYSTEM

Recall from Chapter 1 that the DOS System diskette contains a complete set of the disk operating system programs. This means that programs for both internal and external DOS commands can be loaded and executed from this diskette.

The process of starting a computer is referred to as the **boot process**, **booting the system**, or **starting DOS**. The following outline indicates the important steps that occur in the boot process.

1. Insert the DOS System diskette in drive A and close the drive latch.
2. The boot process is initiated in one of two ways.
    a) A **cold start (cold boot)**: Start the computer by turning the computer's power switch from OFF to ON. For some computers the monitor's power may also need to be turned on.
    b) A **warm start (warm boot, system reset** or **restart)**: Hold the Ctrl and Alt keys down while pressing the Del key (Ctrl-Alt-Del). A warm start is normally used to initiate the boot process if the computer's power is already on.

Once the boot process has been initiated, the computer's central processing unit (**CPU**) automatically executes two special programs that permanently reside in its read-only memory (**ROM**).

- The first program performs a short self-test on some of the computer's component parts, checking for certain types of hardware (equipment) failures. The execution of this program is the reason that your computer appears to be doing nothing for several seconds after the boot process is initiated.
- The second program is called the **bootstrap loader** because it "pulls DOS up by the bootstrap." It begins the process of loading DOS into the computer's memory by first loading and then executing a program called the **bootstrap program** from the initial part of the DOS disk. The execution of this program causes DOS's two hidden files (IBMBIO.COM and IBMDOS.COM) and COMMAND.COM to be loaded into memory. DOS is now loaded, and the boot process is complete.

  Note: The initial part of the disk is commonly referred to as the boot record. The **boot record** contains information about the format structure of the disk along with the bootstrap program.

DOS displays its current date followed by a message to enter a new date:

```
Current date is Sun  1-31-1988
Enter new date (mm-dd-yy):
```

3. Press the Enter (Return) key to accept the displayed date as the current system date or enter the current date in the displayed format, where mm denotes the month (1 through 12), dd denotes the day (1 through 31), and yy denotes the last two digits of the year (80 through 99). The three parts of the day may be separated by a dash (-), a slash (/), or a period (.).

   DOS displays its current time followed by a message to enter a new time:

```
Current time is 11:28:11.61
Enter new time:
```

4. Press the Enter (Return) key to accept the displayed time as the current system time or enter the current time in the displayed format using a twenty-four hour clock. The general time format is hh:mm:ss.xx, where hh denotes hours (0 through 23), mm denotes minutes (0 through 59), ss denotes seconds (0 through 59), and xx denotes hundredths of seconds (0 through 99). The hours, minutes, and seconds may be separated by a colon (:) or a period (.). The time 6:45 p.m. would be entered as 18:45. Note that seconds and hundredths of seconds do not have to be included in the entered time. In fact, the hour specification is the only required field when entering the time.

   After the above preliminaries have been completed, DOS sends a multiline message to the screen identifying the version of DOS and copyright information. A typical example might be:

```
The IBM Personal Computer DOS
Version 3.20 (C) Copyright IBM Corp 1981, 1986
             (C) Copyright Microsoft Corp 1981, 1986
A>
```

A> is the system prompt from the DOS command processor. This prompt indicates that the system is at command level and that the current disk drive (default drive) is drive A.

Notes about Booting the System

- Some personal computers contain the hardware that automatically keeps track of the date and time. This feature is commonly referred to as a **real-time clock/calendar** with battery backup (**permanent clock**). If your computer contains a real-time clock/calendar, you do not need to enter the date and time each time you boot the system.
- If the current date and time are not correctly entered into the computer, then the date and time associated with any file that is created or modified during this session will not be correct. This might cause problems in the future when you try to determine the creation date or the last modification date of a particular file.
- If the DOS disk contains a file named AUTOEXEC.BAT, Steps 3 and 4 under Booting the System will be replaced by the execution of the DOS commands in this file. (Use of the AUTOEXEC.BAT file will be covered in Chapter 9.)
- If a fixed disk is used in booting the system, then the system prompt C> will be displayed on your screen in place of the prompt A>, since C is the letter DOS uses to identify a fixed disk.

CHECKING AND CHANGING THE SYSTEM DATE (DATE)

The **DATE** command allows you to check and to change (if necessary) the DOS system date.

1. With A> as the prompt, enter the following DOS command:

   ```
   A>DATE
   ```

   The DATE command displays the following message:

   ```
   Current date is Sun  1-31-88
   Enter new date (mm-dd-yy):
   ```

2. Check the date. If the date is correct, press the Enter key. If the date is not correct, enter the correct date in the displayed format.

CHECKING AND CHANGING THE SYSTEM TIME (TIME)

The **TIME** command allows you to check and to change (if necessary) the DOS system time.

1. With A> as the prompt, enter the following DOS command:

   ```
   A>TIME
   ```

   The TIME Command displays the following message:

   ```
   Current time is 11:59:41.54
   Enter new time:
   ```

2. Check the time. If the time is correct, press the Enter key. If the time is not correct, enter the correct time using a twenty-four hour clock.

Note: If a computer has a real-time clock/calendar with battery backup (permanent clock), then the DOS commands DATE and TIME do not change its settings. DATE and TIME change only the date and time for the current session. To change the date and time of the real-time clock/calendar on most personal computers, you need to choose the setup option on the computer's diagnostic diskette. On some personal computers a real-time clock/calendar command has been added to the DOS System diskette to change its date and time. In DOS Version 3.30 the DATE and TIME commands do change the real-time clock/calendar settings.

MAKING COPIES OF THE DOS DISKETTES (DISKCOPY)

As a general rule you should never use the original copies of the DOS System diskette and the DOS Supplemental Program diskette as working copies. You should make backup copies of these DOS diskettes, store the original copies in a safe place for future reference, and use the backup copies as your regular working diskettes. You can make these backup copies by following the steps outlined in either of the next two sections, depending upon the number of diskette drives that are available in your personal computer. Each of these sections utilizes the **DISKCOPY** commmand, a command that allows you to copy the entire contents of one diskette (**source diskette**) to a second diskette (**target diskette**). Although the DISKCOPY command is easy to use, Chapter 6 states some reasons why you might choose to use other commands to back up your diskettes.

Note: If you are using DOS Version 3.30, follow the steps given in Appendix C to make your working copy of the DOS System diskette.

Making Copies Using Two Diskette Drives

1. Insert the DOS System diskette in drive A.
2. Insert a blank diskette in drive B.
3. Boot the system if it is not already booted.

4. With A> as the prompt, enter the following DOS command:

   ```
   A>DISKCOPY A: B:
   ```

   Since DISKCOPY is an external DOS command, the DISKCOPY program is loaded into memory from the DOS System diskette in drive A. This program will copy everything from the diskette in drive A to the diskette in drive B. The DISKCOPY program displays the following message:

   Insert SOURCE diskette in drive A:

   Insert TARGET diskette in drive B:

   Press any key when ready . . .

5. Press any key (the DOS System diskette is the source diskette, and the blank diskette is the target diskette).

   The DISKCOPY program displays a second message similar to the following:

   Copying 40 tracks
   9 Sectors/Track, 2 Side(s)

   A short time later the following message may be displayed:

   Formatting while copying . . .

   When the diskette is copied (about one minute), the DISKCOPY program displays the message:

   Copy another diskette (Y/N)?

6. Press the Y key.
7. Remove the target diskette from drive B and label it

   ```
   IBM PC-DOS, Version X.xx, System  or
   MS-DOS, Version X.xx, System
   ```

   where X.xx denotes your DOS version number. This diskette becomes your working copy of the DOS System diskette.

8. Remove the original DOS System diskette from drive A and store it in a safe place.
9. Insert the DOS Supplemental Programs diskette in drive A.
10. Insert a blank diskette in drive B.
11. Press any key.

    When the copy is complete, the following message is displayed:

    Copy another diskette (Y/N)?

12. Press the N key.

    Control is now back at command level, and DOS responds with the A> prompt.

13. Remove the target diskette from drive B and label it

    ```
    IBM PC-DOS, Version X.xx, Supplemental Programs  or
    MS-DOS, Version X.xx, Supplemental Programs
    ```

where X.xx denotes your DOS version number. This diskette becomes your working copy of the DOS Supplemental Programs diskette.

14. Remove the original DOS Supplemental Programs diskette from drive A and store it in a safe place with the DOS System diskette.

Making Copies Using One Diskette Drive

1. Insert the DOS System diskette in drive A.
2. Boot the system if it is not already booted.
3. With A> as the prompt, enter the following DOS command:

   ```
   A>DISKCOPY A:
   ```

   Since DISKCOPY is an external DOS command, the DISKCOPY program is loaded into memory from the DOS System diskette in drive A. This program will make a duplicate copy of a diskette using only drive A. The DISKCOPY program displays the following message:

   ```
   Insert the SOURCE diskette in drive A:
   Press any key when ready . . .
   ```

4. Press any key (the DOS System diskette is the source diskette and is already in drive A).

   The DISKCOPY program displays a second message similar to the following:

   ```
   Copying 40 tracks
   9 Sectors/Track, 2 Side(s)
   ```

   The DISKCOPY program reads as much information from the DOS System diskette as it can into memory. A short time later the following message requests that the diskette in drive A be exchanged:

   ```
   Insert TARGET diskette in drive A:
   Press any key when ready . . .
   ```

5. Remove the DOS System diskette from drive A.
6. Insert a blank (target) diskette in drive A.
7. Press any key.

   After a short delay, the following message may be displayed:

   ```
   Formatting while copying . . .
   ```

   The information from the DOS System (source) diskette that was read and saved in memory is now copied onto the blank (target) diskette. If the DOS diskette has not been completely copied, the following message is displayed:

   ```
   Insert SOURCE diskette in drive A:
   Press any key when ready . . .
   ```

8. Remove the blank (target) diskette from drive A.
9. Insert the DOS System diskette in drive A.
10. Press any key.

You should follow the DISKCOPY messages for exchanging the source (DOS System) diskette and the target diskette until the DOS System diskette is completely copied. When this occurs, the following message is displayed:

Copy another diskette (Y/N)?

11. Press the Y key.
12. Remove the target diskette from drive A and label it

    ```
    IBM PC-DOS, Version X.xx, System  or
    MS-DOS, Version X.xx, System
    ```

    where X.xx denotes your DOS version number. This diskette becomes your working copy of the DOS System diskette. The original DOS System diskette should be stored in a safe place.
13. Insert the DOS Supplemental Programs diskette in drive A.
14. Press any key.

    The DISKCOPY program displays some information about the source diskette and then gives a prompt for a target diskette.
15. Remove the DOS Supplemental Programs diskette from drive A.
16. Insert a blank (target) diskette in drive A.
17. Press any key.

    You should follow the DISKCOPY messages for exchanging the source (DOS Supplemental Programs) diskette and the target (blank) diskette until the DOS Supplemental Programs diskette is completely copied. When this occurs, the following message is displayed:

    Copy another diskette (Y/N)?
18. Press the N key.

    Control is now back to command level, and DOS responds with the A> prompt.
19. Remove the target diskette from drive A and label it

    ```
    IBM PC-DOS, Version X.xx, Supplemental Programs  or
    MS-DOS, Version X.xx, Supplemental Programs
    ```

    where X.xx denotes your DOS version number. This diskette becomes your working copy of the DOS Supplemental Programs diskette. The original DOS Supplemental Programs diskette should be stored in a safe place with the DOS System diskette.

Notes about Making Backup Copies of DOS Diskettes

- Once a working copy of the DOS System diskette has been made, future references to the DOS System diskette mean the working copy of the DOS System diskette.
- You should be very careful about using a 1.2MB diskette drive to generate backup copies of 360KB diskettes. Drive A on an IBM PC AT and on AT

compatibles is a 1.2MB diskette drive. (More attention is given to this subject in Chapters 3 and 6.)

- You might also be wise to make working copies of the Diagnostics and/or Setup diskettes that normally come with a personal computer.
- A more complete discussion about backing up diskettes and files is given in Chapter 6.

Note: Installing DOS on a fixed disk is much more involved than making working copies of the DOS System diskette. The information dealing with the setup and use of a fixed disk is covered in Chapters 3 and 8.

CHANGING THE CURRENT DISK DRIVE (d:)

When the system is at command level and drive A is the default disk drive, DOS displays the prompt A>. If you want to change the default drive to a different drive, enter the letter identifying the drive followed by a colon (:).

1. With A> as the prompt, enter B: to change the default drive to drive B.

```
A>B:
B>
```

2. Enter C: (if you have a fixed disk) to change the default drive to drive C.

```
B>C:
C>
```

3. Enter A: to change the default drive back to drive A.

```
C>A:
A>
```

Note: If a disk drive specification is used for a disk drive that is not installed (for example, C: on a computer without a fixed disk) or not a valid drive specifier (for example, T:), DOS displays the following message:

```
Invalid drive specification
```

CLEARING THE SCREEN (CLS)

The **CLS** (CLear Screen) command allows you to clear all displayed information from the screen except the system prompt, which appears in the upper left-hand corner of the screen.

1. With A> as the prompt, enter the following DOS command:

```
A>CLS
```

DETERMINING DOS VERSION (VER)

The **VER** (VERsion) command allows you to display the version of DOS that you are using.

1. With A> as the prompt, enter the following DOS command:

   ```
   A>VER
   ```

   The VER command displays the following message:

   IBM Personal Computer DOS Version 3.20

3 Preparing a New Disk for Use

The material in this chapter shows you how to prepare a disk for use on your personal computer. The FORMAT and SYS commands are used in the preparation of diskettes and a fixed disk, while the FDISK command is used only with the preparation of a fixed disk. FORMAT, SYS, and FDISK are external DOS commands.

FORMATTING A DISK

Disks are used as a medium upon which information is electronically stored. Before you can use a new disk to store information, you must format the disk with the **FORMAT** command. Formatting a disk allows DOS to find those parts of the disk that are free to receive new information and to find information that was previously placed on the disk. Formatting a new disk is similar to systematically assigning numbers to new mail boxes in a post office. If no addresses (numbers) are assigned to the new post office boxes, postal workers cannot successfully distribute mail through these boxes. Formatting a disk allows DOS to use the disk to save (write to the disk) and retrieve (read from the disk) information.

Characteristics of Unformatted and Formatted Disks

Figure 3.1 illustrates a diskette that has not been formatted. Notice that no addressing has been established on the diskette to allow DOS to save (write) and retrieve (read) information from its surface. Figure 3.2 illustrates a diskette that has been formatted.

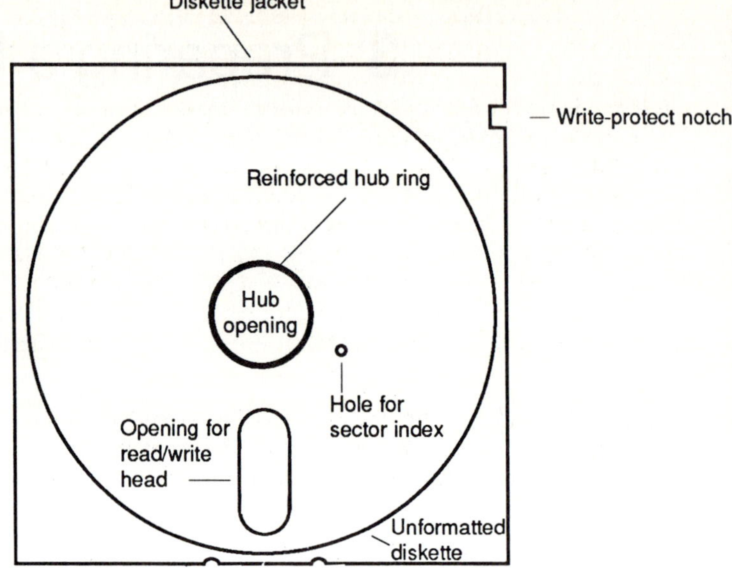

Figure 3.1 Unformatted 5.25 Inch Diskette

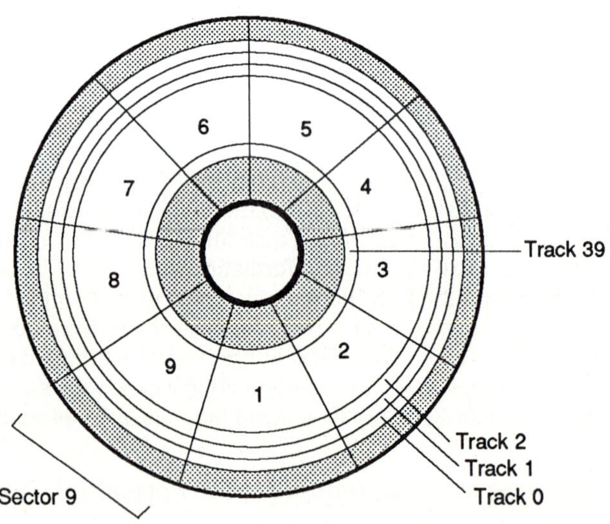

Figure 3.2 Formatted 5.25 Inch 360KB Diskette

Although Figs. 3.1 and 3.2 illustrate properties of unformatted and formatted 5.25 inch diskettes, similar properties hold for all types of disks, including fixed disks. For this reason the remarks in the remainder of this section are made about disks in general.

A formatted disk is divided into narrow concentric circles called **tracks**. Tracks are subdivided into smaller areas called **sectors**; each sector can hold 512 bytes of information. DOS uses the disk side, track, and sector numbers to save and retrieve information; that is, usable areas of a disk's surface are addressed by using the side, track, and sector numbers. The number of tracks and sectors that are created on a formatted disk is determined by the version of DOS that you use, the type of disk drive that is used in the formatting process, and the parameters that are used in the FORMAT command. For information about capacity characteristics of different types of diskettes, you should refer to Table B.2 under the FORMAT command in Appendix B.

Note: If a sticker (**write-protect tab**) is placed over the write-protect notch on a diskette jacket, a diskette drive can read information from the diskette but cannot write information to the diskette. The diskette is said to be **write protected**.

Results of the FORMAT Command

The FORMAT command does five things to a disk to prepare it for use by DOS.

- First, it addresses the usable area of the disk by writing electronic guidelines on the surface of the disk as outlined in Fig. 3.2. These guidelines allow DOS to locate a particular area of the disk by using the side, track, and sector numbers (addresses).
- Second, FORMAT writes on each sector of the disk to determine whether it is free of defects. Bad or defective sectors are marked as write-protected so that you cannot use the bad parts of the disk to store data.
- Third, FORMAT creates a **directory** (main or root directory) for the disk, which contains information about files stored on the disk. This information consists of the filename, the filename extension, the file size in bytes, the date and time the file was created or last updated, and the location (address) of the beginning of the file data on the disk.
- Fourth, FORMAT sets up the **file allocation table (FAT).** This table contains the information to keep track of bad tracks on the disk, to identify which sectors belong to which files, and to identify which sectors are not being used (free). The file allocation table may be thought of as an index to the disk.
- Fifth, FORMAT places a copy of the **boot record** on the first sector of the disk (side 0, track 0, sector 1). The boot record contains information about the format structure of the disk along with the bootstrap program.

Consequently, the FORMAT command identifies five types of sectors on a formatted disk. These sector types are boot record, file allocation table sectors, directory sectors, bad or defective sectors, and data sectors (where file data are stored). The boot record, the file allocation table sectors, and the directory sectors are considered to be disk overhead on a formatted disk.

PREPARING DATA DISKETTES (FORMAT)

This section outlines the steps that are necessary to prepare (format, initialize) a diskette so that it can be used for data storage. This process uses the DOS FORMAT command.

WARNING: FORMAT is one of the most dangerous DOS commands and should be used with great caution. Any data residing on a diskette will be destroyed by the formatting process. Before you format a diskette, you should be sure that there are no valuable data on the diskette.

Formatting a Diskette Using Two Diskette Drives

1. Insert the DOS System diskette in drive A.
2. Insert a blank (target) diskette in drive B.
3. With A> as the prompt, enter the following DOS command:

   ```
   A>FORMAT B:
   ```

   Since FORMAT is an external DOS command, the FORMAT program is loaded into memory from the DOS System diskette in drive A, and then it displays the following message:

   ```
   Insert new diskette for drive B:
   and strike ENTER when ready
   ```

4. Press the Enter key.

   As the diskette is being formatted, the head number (indicating bottom [0] or top [1] of the diskette) and cylinder number (indicating the track number on the bottom or top of the diskette) are displayed. When the formatting process is complete, FORMAT displays the following message:

   ```
   Format complete

       362496 bytes total disk space
       362496 bytes available on disk

   Format another (Y/N)?
   ```

5. Enter Y.
6. Remove your formatted diskette from drive B and insert another blank diskette.

   After formatting several diskettes, enter N to terminate the formatting process. Control is now back at command level, and DOS responds with the A> prompt.

Formatting a Diskette Using One Diskette Drive

1. Insert the DOS System diskette in drive A.
2. With A> as the prompt, enter the following DOS command:

   ```
   A>FORMAT A:
   ```

   After the FORMAT program is loaded into memory from the DOS System diskette in drive A, it displays the following message:

   ```
   Insert new diskette for drive A:
   and strike ENTER when ready
   ```

3. Remove the DOS System diskette from drive A, insert a blank (target) diskette in drive A, and press the Enter key.

   The remainder of the formatting process follows the same steps that were outlined for two diskette drives.

Notes about Formatting Diskettes

- You should always have several formatted diskettes available for immediate use. The first time you lose data because your data diskette is full and will accept no more information, and you do not have a formatted diskette available for use, you will understand the true value of having formatted diskettes readily available.
- If the FORMAT program finds bad sectors on a diskette, it will display a message similar to the following:

  ```
  Format complete
      362496 bytes total disk space
        5120 bytes in bad sectors
      357376 bytes available on disk
  ```

  As a general rule, do not use diskettes that contain bad sectors. Not only do bad sectors decrease the space available to store information, they also raise a question about the quality of the diskette.
- When the FORMAT command is used without any formatting specifications to format a diskette, the diskette drive type dictates the diskette format. That is, a 360KB diskette drive formats a 360KB diskette, and a 1.2MB diskette drive formats a 1.2MB diskette unless the FORMAT command specifies an alternate diskette format.
- If you are using a computer system with a 1.2MB (high-density) diskette drive, you need to be careful how you use 360KB (double-sided) diskettes in the 1.2MB drive. A 1.2MB diskette drive can read and write on a 360KB diskette. 360KB diskettes written on by a 1.2MB drive can be reliably read in another 1.2MB drive, but they may not be reliably read in a 360KB diskette drive.
- There are FORMAT parameters that allow you to specify different capacities of a formatted diskette. For example, you can format a diskette on only one

side (single-sided) or eight sectors per track. For more information about these options you should refer to the FORMAT command in Appendix B.

PREPARING BOOTABLE DISKETTES (FORMAT /S)

The previous section showed you how to format a diskette. However, you cannot boot your system with a diskette that has only been formatted. In order for you to boot your system from a diskette, the diskette must contain the three DOS system files. That is, a bootable diskette must contain the hidden system files IBMBIO.COM and IBMDOS.COM and the visible system file COMMAND.COM.

The advantage of putting DOS on your diskettes is that it allows you to boot your system from any of your diskettes. The disadvantage of having DOS on a diskette is that it takes up some of the diskette's usable space. As a general rule you might want to put DOS on your program diskettes but not on your data diskettes.

Preparing a Bootable Diskette Using Two Diskette Drives

1. Insert the DOS System diskette in drive A.
2. Insert a blank (target) diskette in drive B.
3. With A> as the prompt, enter the following DOS command:

   ```
   A>FORMAT B:/S
   ```

   After the FORMAT program is loaded into memory from the DOS System diskette in drive A, it displays the following message:

   ```
   Insert new diskette for drive B:
   and strike ENTER when ready
   ```

   The /S parameter instructs the FORMAT program to copy the three DOS system files from the diskette in drive A to the target diskette in drive B.
4. Press the Enter key.

   When the formatting process is complete, FORMAT displays the message:

   ```
   Format complete
   System transferred

       362496 bytes total disk space
        69632 bytes used by system
       292864 bytes available on disk

   Format another (Y/N)?
   ```
5. Enter Y and follow the prompts to format another bootable diskette.

   Enter N to terminate the formatting process and return to command level with the A> prompt.

Preparing a Bootable Diskette Using One Diskette Drive

1. Insert the DOS System diskette in drive A.
2. With A> as the prompt, enter the following DOS command:

   ```
   A>FORMAT A:/S
   ```

   After the FORMAT program is loaded into memory from the DOS System diskette in drive A, it displays the following message:

   Insert new diskette for drive A:
   and strike ENTER when ready

3. Remove the DOS System diskette from drive A, insert a blank (target) diskette in drive A, and press the Enter key.

   The remainder of the formatting process follows the same steps that were outlined for two diskette drives.

Transferring DOS to a Formatted Diskette (SYS)

The /S option on the FORMAT command is not the only method for creating a bootable diskette. The following steps outline a process for installing the three DOS system files on a formatted diskette that contains no volume label and no files. The **SYS** (SYStem) command is used to copy the two DOS hidden files to a diskette. For this process to work, the formatted diskette must have an empty directory or the diskette must have been originally formatted with the /S or /B parameter. (See the FORMAT command in Appendix B for information about the /B parameter.)

1. Insert the DOS System diskette in drive A.
2. Insert a formatted diskette (with an empty directory) in drive B.
3. With A> as the prompt, enter the following DOS command:

   ```
   A>SYS B:
   ```

   After the SYS program is loaded into memory from the DOS System diskette in drive A, it checks the directory of the diskette in drive B. If the directory of the diskette in drive B is empty, SYS instructs DOS to copy the two DOS hidden files IBMBIO.COM and IBMDOS.COM from the DOS System diskette in drive A to the diskette in drive B. When this process is complete, SYS displays the following message before returning to command level with the A> prompt:

   System transferred

4. Enter the following DOS command:

   ```
   A>COPY COMMAND.COM B:
   ```

   This command copies the DOS file COMMAND.COM from the DOS System diskette in drive A to the diskette in drive B. When this process is complete, COPY displays the following message before returning to command level with the A> prompt:

   1 File(s) copied

Since the diskette in drive B now contains the three DOS system files, it is a bootable diskette.

Note: A comprehensive discussion of the COPY command is given in Chapter 5.

FORMATTING A DISKETTE WITH A VOLUME LABEL (FORMAT /V)

You might want to put a **volume label** (name) in the directory of a diskette to help you identify the diskette. The following steps show how this can be done on a system with two diskette drives.

1. Insert the DOS System diskette in drive A.
2. Insert a blank (target) diskette in drive B.
3. With A> as the prompt, enter the following DOS command:

   ```
   A>FORMAT B:/V
   ```

   If you want to put a label on a bootable diskette, enter the following DOS command:

   ```
   A>FORMAT B:/S/V
   ```

   The /V parameter instructs the FORMAT program to prompt you for a volume label.
4. Press the Enter key after FORMAT prompts you to insert a new diskette in drive B.

   After the diskette in drive B is formatted and the DOS system files are transferred to it, FORMAT displays the following message:

   ```
   Format complete
   System transferred
   Volume label (11 characters, ENTER for none)?
   ```
5. Enter the following volume label (or one of your choice) after the above prompt:

   ```
   SAMPLE-DISK
   ```

   A volume label consists of one to eleven valid filename characters plus a space. If you press the Enter key without entering any characters, no volume label will be put on the diskette.
6. Enter Y to format another diskette with a volume label.

   Enter N to terminate the formatting process and return to command level with the A> prompt.

PREPARING A FIXED DISK FOR USE WITH DOS

This section will show you how to prepare your system's fixed disk (hard disk) so that you can boot DOS from it and so that DOS can use it. Four things must be done to your fixed disk before you can effectively use it.

- First, you must identify your fixed disk to DOS with the **FDISK** (Fixed DISK) command. The FDISK command can actually be used to divide (partition) your fixed disk into sections (partitions) so that different operating systems can use it. In fact, the primary purpose of the FDISK command is to create and manage partitions on a fixed disk. The discussion in this section will be limited to partitioning the entire fixed disk to DOS.
- Second, the fixed disk must be formatted.
- Third, the DOS system files must be placed on the fixed disk so that you can boot your system from this disk.
- Fourth, the external DOS command files and the DOS utility program files need to be copied onto the fixed disk so that they will be conveniently available for you to use.

WARNING: If your fixed disk is already identified to DOS, is formatted, and contains the DOS programs, you should not repeat these steps. A comprehensive discussion on using a fixed disk is given in Chapter 8.

Identifying a Fixed Disk to DOS (FDISK)

1. Insert the DOS System diskette in drive A.
2. With A> as the prompt, enter the following DOS command:

   ```
   A>FDISK
   ```

   After the FDISK program is loaded into memory from the DOS System diskette in drive A, it displays a list of four FDISK options on the screen.
3. Choose the first option, *Create DOS Partition*, by entering a 1.

   If a DOS partition already exists on your fixed disk, FDISK displays the following message:

   ```
   DOS partition already exists.

   Press Esc to return to FDISK Options
   ```

   In this case, press the Esc key twice and you will return to command level with the A> prompt. Otherwise, FDISK displays the following message:

   ```
   Create DOS Partition

   Do you wish to use the entire fixed
   disk for DOS (Y/N).............?[Y]
   ```

4. Enter Y.

   FDISK now displays the following message:

   ```
   System will now restart
   Insert DOS diskette in drive A:
   Press any key when ready . . .
   ```

5. Press any key.

   DOS is restarted (rebooted), and your fixed disk is now identified to DOS as drive C.

Formatting and Installing DOS on a Fixed Disk (FORMAT /S/V)

1. Insert the DOS System diskette in drive A.
2. With A> as the prompt, enter the following DOS command:

   ```
   A>FORMAT C:/S/V
   ```

   After the FORMAT program is loaded into memory from the DOS System diskette in drive A, it displays the following message:

   ```
   WARNING ALL DATA ON NON-REMOVABLE DISK
   DRIVE C: WILL BE LOST!
   Proceed with Format (Y/N)?
   ```

3. Enter Y.

   As the disk is being formatted, the head number and cylinder number are displayed. When the formatting process is complete, FORMAT displays the following message:

   ```
   Format complete
   System transferred
   Volume label (11 characters, ENTER for none)?
   ```

4. Enter the following string (or one of your choice) for the volume label on your fixed disk:

   ```
   FIXED-DISK
   ```

   FORMAT displays the following message before returning to command level with the A> prompt:

   ```
   31768576 bytes total disk space
      69632 bytes used by the system
   31698944 bytes available on disk
   ```

   Your fixed disk is now formatted; it contains the three DOS system files—IBMBIO.COM, IBMDOS.COM, and COMMAND.COM—and it has FIXED-DISK as its volume label.

Copying DOS External Commands to a Fixed Disk

1. Insert the DOS System diskette in drive A.

2. With A> as the prompt, enter the following DOS command:

```
A>COPY *.* C:
```

This command copies each file from the DOS System diskette in drive A to the fixed disk. Each filename and extension is displayed as it is being copied. After all of the files have been copied, COPY displays the following message before returning to command level with the A> prompt:

```
39 File(s) copied
```

3. Remove the DOS System diskette from drive A.
4. Insert the DOS Supplemental Programs diskette in drive A.
5. Enter the following DOS command:

```
A>COPY *.* C:
```

This command copies each file from the DOS Supplemental Programs diskette in drive A to the fixed disk. After all of the files have been copied, control returns to command level with the A> prompt.

Note: A comprehensive discussion of the COPY command is given in Chapter 5.

Booting Your System from a Fixed Disk

At this point your fixed disk should be formatted and should contain a copy of all files that are on the DOS System diskette and the DOS Supplemental Programs diskette. Consequently, your system, like most systems, should automatically boot from your fixed disk if there is no diskette in drive A.

1. Make sure no diskette is in drive A.
2. Press Ctrl-Alt-Del to boot the system.

Note that your system boots from your fixed disk. After you respond to the date and time prompts, your system is at command level with the C> prompt.

Note: You should store your two DOS diskettes and use your fixed disk to boot your system and to access any external DOS commands that you want to use. Remember that a comprehensive discussion on using a fixed disk is given in Chapter 8.

4 Displaying Information about a Diskette/Disk

Recall from Chapter 3 that a disk directory is created by the FORMAT command during the formatting process and serves as a table of contents for the information stored on the disk. Since information stored on a disk is stored as a file, DOS keeps track of this information through file entries in a directory. There are four DOS commands that are designed to tell you what is on a disk. These commands are DIR, CHKDSK, VOL, and LABEL. DIR and VOL are internal DOS commands, while CHKDSK and LABEL are external DOS commands. The SORT command, an external DOS command, is also presented in this chapter.

DISPLAYING THE TABLE OF CONTENTS (DIRECTORY INFORMATION) OF A DISK

The **DIR** (DIRectory) command is used to display the contents of a disk's directory. This displayed information begins with a heading that includes the volume label of the disk (if it has one) and the directory's path specification. At this point the path specification consists of the drive designator followed by a reverse slash (\). Path specifications are covered in detail in Chapter 8. Listed under the directory heading is the following information for each named file: the filename and extension, the size of the file in bytes, and the date and time that the file was created or last modified. After all named files in a directory are listed, a summary line is displayed that states the number of files that were listed and the number of free bytes that are available for use on the disk. Figure 4.1 contains a sample directory listing. For the remainder of this chapter you can assume that the information in Fig. 4.1 came from the diskette called SAMPLE-DISK.

Displaying Complete Directory Information (DIR)

The DIR command can be used to display the entire contents of a disk's directory by specifying a particular disk drive in the DIR command.

1. Insert the DOS System diskette in drive A.
2. With A> as the prompt, enter the following DOS command:

   ```
   A>DIR A:
   ```

   The DIR command instructs DOS to display the complete directory information of the diskette in drive A. Figure 4.1 shows the result of this command as if SAMPLE-DISK was in drive A.
3. Remove the DOS System diskette from drive A and insert it in drive B.
4. With A> as the prompt, enter the following DOS command:

   ```
   A>DIR B:
   ```

   This command instructs DOS to display the directory entries for the diskette in drive B.

```
 Volume in drive A is SAMPLE-DISK
 Directory of  A:\

COMMAND  COM    23791  12-30-85  12:00p
TREE     COM     3357  12-30-85  12:00p
FIND     EXE     6416  12-30-85  12:00p
FORMAT   COM    11135  12-30-85  12:00p
APPNDA   DOC    11776   7-15-87  10:49p
WSFORM   WKS    17024   9-16-86  10:43p
APPNDC   DOC     4096   1-31-88  10:52p
BUDGET88 WKS     9216  12-03-87  11:34p
BUDGFORM WKS     5888   8-29-86  12:41a
APPNDA   ASC    10752   8-08-87  11:03p
APPNDC           2816   1-31-88  11:13p
FONT2    DOC     1536   5-06-87   1:35a
FONT11   DOC     1536   8-04-87  12:21a
APPNDA           3216  10-26-87  11:12p
APPND            7936   3-05-88  11:22p
       15 File(s)    120832 bytes free
```

Figure 4.1 Directory Listing for SAMPLE-DISK

Pausing after Each Screen Image (DIR /P)

You probably noticed that one problem with displaying the directory information from the DOS System diskette is that it cannot all be displayed in one screen image. Some of the directory information scrolls off of the top of the screen before it can be read. There are two ways to pause the output to the screen so that you will have time to read it. One method involves sending an interrupt message to DOS instructing it to suspend output to the screen until it receives a continue message. This is accomplished by entering Ctrl-S (hold the Ctrl key down and press the S key). Output to the screen immediately stops but will continue when any key is pressed. (Note that Ctrl-S and Ctrl-NumLock have similar effects in this situation.) The second method involves using the pause (/P) parameter in the DIR command.

1. Insert the DOS System diskette in drive A.
2. With A> as the prompt, enter the following DOS command:

   ```
   A>DIR /P
   ```

   Note that you do not need to specify A: in the DIR command (DIR A: /P), since drive A is the default drive.

   The /P parameter instructs the DIR command to pause the directory output listing after a full screen of directory entries is displayed. After a full screen of directory information is displayed, the directory output pauses, and the DIR command displays the following message:

   ```
   Strike a key when ready . . .
   ```

3. Press any key.

   The directory entries continue to be displayed on the screen, pausing each time the screen is filled with new information. This process may be repeated several times for directories with a large number of entries.

Displaying Abbreviated Directory Information (DIR /W)

The DIR command can be used to display a disk's directory in an abbreviated form by using the /W parameter in the DIR command.

1. Insert the DOS System diskette in drive A.
2. With A> as the prompt, enter the following DOS command:

   ```
   A>DIR /W
   ```

   The /W parameter instructs the DIR command to display only the file names and extensions in a wide-line format. Figure 4.2 shows the result of this command as if SAMPLE-DISK was in drive A.

```
Volume in drive A is SAMPLE-DISK
Directory of  A:\

COMMAND  COM    TREE     COM   FIND      EXE   FORMAT   COM   APPNDA   DOC
WSFORM   WKS    APPNDC   DOC   BUDGET88  WKS   BUDGFORM WKS   APPDNA   ASC
APPNDC          FONT2    DOC   FONT11    DOC   APPNDA         APPND
       15 File(s)   120832 bytes free
```

Figure 4.2 Wide Format Directory Listing for SAMPLE-DISK

Displaying Directory Information for Selected Files

The DIR command can be used to display directory information about a single file or about groups of files having similar filenames and/or extensions. The wildcard characters * and ? (introduced in Chapter 1) are used extensively to specify groups of files in the DIR command. Table 4.1 illustrates the results of the DIR command when used with different file specifications containing wildcard characters.

DISPLAYING DIRECTORY INFORMATION IN ALPHABETICAL ORDER (DIR ¦ SORT)

Sometimes you might want to have the directory entries displayed in alphabetical order. This can be accomplished by **piping** (sending) the output from the DIR command to the **SORT** command as input. The SORT command sorts each line of output from the DIR command into alphabetical order. The symbol ¦ is used to specify piping in the DOS command sequence. (Note that the symbol ¦ is normally located above the backslash (\) on the keyboard.)

1. Insert the DOS System diskette in drive A.
2. Insert a formatted nonblank diskette whose directory you wish to list in drive B.
3. With A> as the prompt, enter the following DOS command:

   ```
   A>DIR B: ¦ SORT
   ```

   The output information generated by the DIR B: command is piped as input to the SORT program, which is loaded from the DOS System diskette in drive A. The directory information is sorted and then displayed in alphabetical order on the screen. Figure 4.3 shows the result of this command as if SAMPLE-DISK was in drive B.

TABLE 4.1 EXAMPLE DIR COMMANDS WITH SPECIFIED FILES

(Assume that you are using the directory of SAMPLE-DISK in Fig. 4.1. That is, assume that A> is the prompt and that the diskette SAMPLE-DISK is in drive A.)

Requested Action	Example Command	File Names Listed	
List a single file name	A>DIR WSFORM.WKS	WSFORM	WKS
List all file names beginning with the same first character and having any extension	A>DIR F*	FIND	EXE
		FORMAT	COM
		FONT2	DOC
		FONT11	DOC
List all file names beginning with the same first few characters and having any extension	A>DIR BUDG*.*	BUDGET88	WKS
		BUDGFORM	WKS
List all file names having no extension	A>DIR *.	APPNDC	
		APPNDA	
		APPND	
List all file names having the same extension	A>DIR *.WKS	WSFORM	WKS
		BUDGET88	WKS
		BUDGFORM	WKS
List all file names having the same filename and any extension	A>DIR APPNDA.*	APPNDA	DOC
		APPNDA	ASC
		APPNDA	
List all file names beginning with the same first five characters, having at most six characters in the filename, and having any extension	A>DIR APPND?	APPNDA	DOC
		APPNDC	DOC
		APPNDA	ASC
		APPNDC	
		APPNDA	
		APPND	

```
        15 File(s)    120832 bytes free
 Directory of  B:\
 Volume in drive B is SAMPLE-DISK
APPND              7936   3-05-88  11:22p
APPNDA            73216  10-26-87  11:12p
APPNDA   ASC      10752   8-08-87  11:03p
APPNDA   DOC      11776   7-15-87  10:49p
APPNDC             2816   1-31-88  11:13p
APPNDC   DOC       4096   1-31-88  10:52p
BUDGET88 WKS       9216  12-03-87  11:34p
BUDGFORM WKS       5888   8-29-86  12:41a
COMMAND  COM      23791  12-30-85  12:00p
FIND     EXE       6416  12-30-85  12:00p
FONT11   DOC       1536   8-04-87  12:21a
FONT2    DOC       1536   5-06-87   1:35a
FORMAT   COM      11135  12-30-85  12:00p
TREE     COM       3357  12-30-85  12:00p
WSFORM   WKS      17024   9-16-86  10:43p
```

Figure 4.3 Sorted Directory Listing for SAMPLE-DISK

SENDING DIRECTORY INFORMATION TO THE PRINTER (DIR > PRN)

Many times you want a **hard copy** (printed copy) of the directory listing for a disk. Since the standard output device on an IBM PC is the display screen, you must instruct DOS to **redirect** (send) the output from the DIR command to the printer. This is accomplished by using the **output redirection symbol >** in the DOS command sequence.

1. Insert the DOS System diskette in drive A.
2. Ready your printer.
3. With A> as the prompt, enter the following DOS command:

   ```
   A>DIR > PRN
   ```

   The redirection symbol > instructs DOS to send the output from the DIR command to the printer that is specified by PRN. You will notice that the directory information is not displayed on the screen but is printed on the printer. When the printing is completed, DOS returns to command level with the A> prompt.

SENDING ALPHABETIZED DIRECTORY INFORMATION TO THE PRINTER (DIR ¦ SORT > PRN)

The piping and redirection features may be combined to give you a printed directory listing in alphabetical order.

1. Insert the DOS System diskette in drive A.
2. Insert a formatted nonblank diskette whose directory you wish to list in drive B.
3. Ready your printer.
4. With A> as the prompt, enter the following DOS command:

   ```
   A>DIR B: ¦ SORT > PRN
   ```

   The output from the DIR B: command is piped as input to the SORT program, which is loaded into memory from the DOS System diskette in drive A. After the directory information is sorted in alphabetical order, the sorted information is redirected to your printer for printing.

Note: When the piping feature is utilized, DOS generates temporary files on the disk in the default drive to store the input and output data being piped. Consequently, the disk in the default drive cannot be write protected when you use piping in a DOS command sequence.

CHECKING A DISKETTE/DISK (CHKDSK)

Even though the DIR command displays a great deal of information about the contents of a disk, it does not give you a complete picture of what is stored on a disk. The **CHKDSK** (CHecK DiSK) command must be used to display certain important characteristics of a disk that are not displayed by the DIR command. In fact, the CHKDSK command does several things for you.

- First, CHKDSK analyzes the directory of the specified disk, comparing the directory entries with the locations and lengths of the files. It reports any errors that it finds.
- Second, CHKDSK displays information about how the disk space is being utilized. Information about bad sectors (if they exist) is also reported to you.
- Third, CHKDSK displays a report on the amount of memory available in your system.
- Fourth, CHKDSK can be used to display the file names of both user and hidden files on a disk.

1. Insert the DOS System diskette in drive A.
2. With A> as the prompt, enter the following DOS command:

   ```
   A>CHKDSK A:
   ```

After the CHKDSK program is loaded into memory from the DOS System diskette in drive A, it analyzes the disk in the specified or default drive—in this case, drive A. Note that the drive specifier A: in the above command is not necessary, since drive A is the default drive. To check a disk in drive B, you would have to specify B: in the CHKDSK command. When CHKDSK completes the check disk process, the following information is displayed:

```
362496 bytes total disk space
 45056 bytes in 3 hidden files
294912 bytes in 39 user files
 22528 bytes available on disk

655360 bytes total memory
609024 bytes free
```

This status report tells you that there are thirty-nine user files and three hidden files on the diskette. Recall that the DIR command listed all of the user files for you but gave you no information about any hidden files. To obtain a complete list of both user and hidden files on a disk, in addition to the information outlined above, you should use the view (/V) parameter of the CHKDSK command.

3. With A> as the prompt, enter the following DOS command:

   ```
   A>CHKDSK /V
   ```

   Note that the two DOS hidden files, IBMBIO.COM and IBMDOS.COM, are the first two entries of the displayed directory list.

CHECKING FILES (CHKDSK filespec)

CHKDSK can also be used to check the way files are stored on a disk. The CHKDSK command will tell you whether a file is stored on a disk in a contiguous manner (contiguous or adjacent sectors) or stored in disjoint (separated) blocks (sectors). A file is called **fragmented** if it is stored on a disk in nonadjacent sectors. A disk drive uses more time to read and write fragmented files than it does to access files stored on contiguous sectors.

1. Insert the DOS System diskette in drive A.
2. Insert a formatted nonblank diskette that you want to check in drive B.
3. With A> as the prompt, enter the following DOS command:

   ```
   A>CHKDSK B:*.*
   ```

   If any file on the diskette in drive B is fragmented, a message similar to the following will be displayed:

   ```
   B:\filename.ext
   Contains 4 non-contiguous blocks.
   ```

   Diskettes that have a lot of file creation and deletion activity become fragmented, since disk space is not allocated sequentially. The first free sector that DOS finds is the next sector allocated to a file, regardless of its location on the diskette. Disk fragmentation can be eliminated through the use of the COPY and XCOPY commands. (Refer to Chapter 6.)

Note: You should periodically use the CHKDSK command to check the disks that you use regularly. This procedure will keep you informed of any problem areas that have developed on a disk.

DISKETTE/DISK VOLUME LABEL

When you are working with many diskettes, you might want to assign a name to each of your diskettes to assist you with diskette identification. DOS allows you to assign a **volume label** (name) to any fixed disk or diskette. Recall from Chapter 3 that the /V option of the FORMAT command gives you the opportunity to assign a volume label to a disk at the completion of the formatting process. The volume label can be up to eleven characters long, using the same characters that are valid for filenames plus a space.

Displaying a Volume Label (VOL)

The **VOL** (VOLume) command allows you to display the volume identification label of the disk in the specified or default drive.

1. Insert the DOS System diskette in drive A.
2. With A> as the prompt, enter the following DOS command:

   ```
   A>VOL A:
   ```

   The VOL command looks for a volume label in the directory of the diskette in the specified drive—in this case, drive A—and displays the following message:

   ```
   Volume in drive A has no label
   ```

   If the diskette in drive A had contained the volume label SYSTEM-DISK, then the VOL command would have displayed the following message:

   ```
   Volume in drive A is SYSTEM-DISK
   ```

   Note that the drive specifier A: in the above command is not necessary since drive A is the default drive.

Creating, Changing, and Removing a Volume Label (LABEL)

This section shows you how to assign a volume label to a disk that has been formatted without one, change a volume label that was previously assigned to a disk, and remove a volume label from a disk. The **LABEL** command allows you to perform each of these functions to a disk.

Note: The LABEL command was introduced in DOS Version 3.0 and is not available in previous versions of DOS.

1. Insert the DOS System diskette in drive A.

2. With A> as the prompt, enter the following DOS command:

```
A>LABEL A:
```

After the LABEL program is loaded into memory from the DOS System diskette in drive A, it displays the following message about the disk in the specified or default disk drive—in this case, drive A:

Volume in drive A has no label

Volume label (11 characters, ENTER for none)?

3. Enter the following characters after the message prompt:

```
SYSTEM-DISK
```

The DOS System diskette is assigned the volume label SYSTEM-DISK.

4. With A> as the prompt, enter the following DOS command:

```
A>VOL
```

The VOL command displays the message:

Volume in drive A is SYSTEM-DISK

5. With A> as the prompt, enter the following DOS command:

```
A>LABEL
```

The LABEL command displays the following message:

Volume in drive A is SYSTEM-DISK

Volume label (11 characters, ENTER for none)?

6. Enter the following characters after the message prompt:

```
DOS SYSTEM
```

This response changed the volume label on the DOS System diskette to DOS SYSTEM.

7. With A> as the prompt, enter the following DOS commmand:

```
A>LABEL
```

The LABEL command displays the following message:

Volume in drive A is DOS SYSTEM

Volume Label (11 characters, ENTER for none)?

8. Press the Enter key.

The LABEL command displays the message:

Delete current volume label (Y/N)?

9. Enter Y.

This response removed the label from your DOS System diskette.

10. With A> as the prompt, enter the following DOS command:

```
A>LABEL A:DOS-SYS-DSK
```

This form of the LABEL command assigns the volume label DOS-SYS-DSK to the diskette in drive A.

11. Insert a data diskette in drive B.
12. With A> as the prompt, enter the following DOS command:

    ```
    A>LABEL B:DATA-DISK
    ```

    The volume label DATA-DISK is assigned to the diskette in drive B. If the diskette in drive B already has a volume label, it is replaced by the new label.

Note: With the new volume label assigned to your DOS System diskette, use the CHKDSK command with the /V option to observe that the volume label DOS-SYS-DSK was entered into the diskette directory as a hidden file entry.

5 Manipulating Files and File Characteristics

In Chapter 3 the COPY command was used to transfer the COMMAND.COM file from the DOS System diskette to another diskette and to transfer the external DOS commands from the DOS System diskette to a fixed disk. The material in this chapter shows you how to make copies of a file (COPY), remove a file name from a disk's directory (DEL, ERASE), change the name and/or extension of a file (RENAME), and modify the attributes of a file (ATTRIB). COPY, RENAME, DEL, and ERASE are internal DOS commands, while ATTRIB is an external DOS command. Note that the material in this chapter deals only with user files.

Recall from Chapter 1 that a file specification normally consists of a filename and an optional filename extension. Sometimes a file specification includes a disk drive specifier and a path name.

COPYING ONE USER FILE (COPY)

The **COPY** command can be used to copy a specified file to the same disk using a different filename and/or extension or to a second disk using the same filename and extension or using a different filename and/or extension.

Copying to the Same Disk, Different Filename and/or Extension

1. Insert the DOS System diskette in drive A.
2. With A> as the prompt, enter the following DOS command:

   ```
   A>COPY A:FORMAT.COM A:FORMAT.BAK
   ```

   The COPY command instructs DOS to copy a single file—in this case, FORMAT.COM—from the diskette in drive A to the diskette in drive A giving it the same filename but a different extension. A:FORMAT.COM is called the **source file specification**, and A:FORMAT.BAK is called the **target file specification**. When the copying process is complete, the following message is displayed:

   ```
           1 File(s) copied
   ```

   Your DOS System diskette now contains two copies of the FORMAT program, the original copy and the newly created backup copy FORMAT.BAK.

   Note: Since drive A is the default drive, you do not need to specify A: in the source and target file specifications in the above COPY command.

3. With A> as the prompt, enter the following DOS command:

   ```
   A>COPY FORMAT.COM FORMAT.COM
   ```

   The COPY command displays the message:

   ```
   File cannot be copied onto itself
           0 File(s) copied
   ```

   This message means that the source and target file specifications in a COPY command cannot specify the same file. For diskettes this usually means that either the target filename or the target filename extension must be different to copy a file onto the same diskette.
4. With A> as the prompt, enter the following DOS command:

   ```
   A>COPY FORMAT.COM FRMT.*
   ```

   The COPY command instructs DOS to copy a single file—in this case, FORMAT.COM—from the diskette in the default drive (drive A) to the diskette in the default drive (drive A) giving the copied file a different filename (FRMT) but the same extension (.COM).

   Note: When the wildcard character * is used in place of a filename (or an extension) in the target file specification of a COPY command, the corresponding filename (or file extension) in the source file specification is substituted for the * character.

Note: Do not worry about the extra files that you just put on your DOS System diskette. You will learn how to remove these files from your directory before the end of this chapter.

Copying to a Second Disk

The COPY command is normally used to copy named files from a disk in one drive (source disk) to a disk in a second drive (target disk) using either the same or different filenames and extensions. The following examples illustrate the use of the COPY command to copy a single specified file from a disk in one drive to a disk in another drive.

1. Insert the DOS System diskette in drive A.
2. Insert a formatted diskette with an empty directory in drive B.
3. With A> as the prompt, enter the following DOS command:

   ```
   A>COPY FORMAT.COM B:FORMAT.COM
   ```

   The COPY command instructs DOS to copy the specified file—in this case, FORMAT.COM—from the diskette in the default drive (drive A) to the diskette in drive B using the same file name. Each of the following commands would have the same result as the above command.

   ```
   A>COPY FORMAT.COM B:FORMAT.*
   A>COPY FORMAT.COM B:*.*
   A>COPY FORMAT.COM B:
   ```

   When you want the target filename and extension to be the same as the source filename and extension, you need to specify only the target drive in the COPY command.
4. Change the default drive to drive B.
5. With B> as the prompt, enter the following DOS command:

   ```
   B>COPY A:FORMAT.COM
   ```

   Since B is the default drive, the COPY command copies the specified file—in this case, FORMAT.COM—from the diskette in drive A to the diskette in the default drive (drive B). When no target file specification is given in the COPY command, the default drive is assumed, and the source filename and extension are used for the target file.
6. With B> as the prompt, enter the following DOS command:

   ```
   B>COPY A:FORMAT.COM FRMT.BAK
   ```

   Since B is the default drive, the COPY command copies the specifed file—in this case, FORMAT.COM—from the diskette in drive A to the diskette in the default drive (drive B) using a different filename and extension.

COPYING SEVERAL FILES (COPY)

Recall from Chapter 4 that the wildcard characters * and ? are used to identify groups of files having similar filenames and/or extensions. The following examples illustrate the use of wildcard characters with the COPY command to copy groups of files having similar file names from a disk in one drive to a disk in a second drive.

1. Insert the DOS System diskette in drive A.
2. Insert a formatted diskette with an empty directory in drive B.
3. With A> as the prompt, enter the following DOS command:

   ```
   A>COPY F*.COM B:
   ```

   This COPY command instructs DOS to copy from the diskette in the default drive (drive A) each file having the same first character in the filename—in this case, F—and the same extension—in this case, .COM—to the diskette in drive B using the same filename and extension. Also note that DOS displays the specification of each copied file when a wildcard character is used in the source file specification of the COPY command.
4. With A> as the prompt, enter the following DOS command:

   ```
   A>COPY F*.* B:
   ```

   The COPY command copies from the diskette in the default drive (drive A) each file having the same first character in the filename—in this case, F—and any extension to the diskette in drive B.
5. Change the default drive to drive B.
6. With B> as the prompt, enter the following DOS command:

   ```
   B>COPY A:F*.*
   ```

   Since drive B is the default drive, it is the implied target drive in the above COPY command. Consequently, this command performs the same tasks that were performed by the COPY command in item 4 above.
7. With B> as the prompt, enter the following DOS command:

   ```
   B>COPY A:*.COM
   ```

   This command copies from the diskette in drive A each file having the same extension—in this case, .COM—to the diskette in the default drive (drive B) using the same filename and extension.
8. With B> as the prompt, enter the following DOS command:

   ```
   B>DIR *.COM
   ```

   The DIR command displays from the diskette's directory in the default drive (drive B) all file names having the same extension—in this case, .COM. Each displayed file was copied to the diskette in drive B by one of the above COPY commands.

9. With B> as the prompt, enter the following DOS command:

```
B>COPY A:*.SYS *.BAK
```

   This command copies from the diskette in drive A each file having the same extension—in this case, .SYS—to the diskette in the default drive (drive B) using the same filename but with .BAK as the new extension.

10. Change the default drive to drive A.
11. With A> as the prompt, enter the following DOS command:

```
A>COPY *.* B:
```

   This command copies each file on the diskette in the default drive (drive A) to the diskette in drive B using the same file name.

Note: If you want to check the quality of a copied file (or files), you should use the /V parameter at the end of the COPY command line. This parameter instructs DOS to verify that the source and target files are identical after copying.

REMOVING (DELETING, ERASING) FILE NAMES FROM A DIRECTORY (DEL, ERASE)

Now that you know how to make copies of files, you need to know how to remove unwanted file names (specifications) from a disk's directory. The **DEL** (DELete) and **ERASE** commands allow you to remove specified files from a directory. Only the DEL command will be used in this section, since both the DEL and ERASE commands perform exactly the same operations.

Removing One File Name from a Directory

The DEL command can be used to delete a single file name from a disk's directory by specifying the file name in the DEL command. Recall from the first part of this chapter that you created two new files on the DOS System diskette. These files were named FORMAT.BAK and FRMT.COM.

1. Insert the DOS System diskette in drive A.
2. With A> as the prompt, enter the following DOS command:

```
A>DEL FORMAT.BAK
```

   The DEL command instructs DOS to remove a single file name—in this case, FORMAT.BAK—from the directory of the diskette in the default drive—in this case, the DOS System diskette in drive A.

3. With A> as the prompt, enter the following DOS command:

```
A>DEL FRMT.COM
```

   This command deletes a single file name—in this case, FRMT.COM—from the directory of the DOS System diskette in drive A.

Now the two extra file names have been deleted from the directory of your DOS System diskette, and it is back to its original form.

4. With A> as the prompt, enter the following DOS command:

```
A>DIR F*
```

The DIR command displays from the diskette in the default drive (drive A) all file names beginning with the same first character—in this case, F.

This verifies that the two extra file names were removed from the disk's directory.

Removing Several File Names from a Directory

The following examples illustrate the use of wildcard characters with the DEL command to delete groups of files having similar file names from the directory of a disk. In each of the examples the first DIR command is used to display the file names that the DEL command will delete from the disk's directory, while the second DIR command verifies that the file names have been deleted from the disk's directory.

1. Insert the DOS System diskette in drive A.
2. Insert a scratch diskette in drive B.
3. With A> as the prompt, enter the following DOS command to create a scratch copy of the DOS System diskette in drive B:

```
A>DISKCOPY A: B:
```

Note: If you are using a computer with only one diskette drive, use the single drive form of the DISKCOPY command that is outlined in Chapter 2. On a single diskette drive system you should insert the scratch copy of the DOS System diskette in drive A and follow the steps given below, ignoring the references to drive B.

4. With A> as the prompt, enter the following DOS commands:

```
A>DIR B:F*.COM
A>DEL B:F*.COM
A>DIR B:F*.COM
```

The DEL command deletes from the diskette's directory in the specified drive (drive B) each file name having the same first character in the filename—in this case, F—and the same extension—in this case, .COM.

5. With A> as the prompt, enter the following DOS commands:

```
A>DIR B:A*.*
A>DEL B:A*.*
A>DIR B:A*.*
```

The DEL command deletes from the diskette's directory in the specified drive (drive B) each file name having the same first character in the filename—in this case, A—and any extension.

6. Change the default drive to drive B.
7. With B> as the prompt, enter the following DOS commands:

```
B>DIR *.EXE
B>DEL *.EXE
B>DIR *.EXE
```

   The DEL command deletes from the diskette's directory in the default drive (drive B) each file name that has the same extension—in this case, .EXE.
8. With B> as the prompt, enter the following DOS commands:

```
B>DIR KEY*.*
B>DEL KEY*.*
B>DIR KEY*.*
```

   The DEL command deletes from the diskette's directory in the default drive (drive B) each file name that has the same first few characters in the filename—in this case, KEY—and any extension.
9. With B> as the prompt, enter the following DOS commands:

```
B>DIR D*
B>DEL D*
```

   The DEL command displays the following message:

   File not found

   Note the difference in the way that D* is interpreted by the DIR and DEL commands. DIR displays from the diskette in the default drive (drive B) each file name having the same first character in the filename—in this case, D—and any extension. The DEL command searches the directory of the diskette in the default drive (drive B) to delete each file having the same first character in the filename—in this case, D—and no extension. Consequently, no files are deleted from the directory. Note that the specification D*. in the DIR command acts like D* or D*. in the DEL command.
10. With B> as the prompt, enter the following DOS commands:

```
B>DIR *.*
B>DEL *.*
B>DIR
```

   Before the DEL command deletes all file names from the diskette's directory in the default drive (drive B), it displays the following message:

   Are you sure (Y/N)?
11. Enter Y to delete all file names from the diskette's directory in drive B.

   Enter N to cancel the DEL command.

CHANGING FILE NAMES (RENAME)

Quite often you create a file with a particular filename and extension and later decide that you want to change the filename and/or extension. The **RENAME** command allows you to rename a file or group of files within the same disk directory. In the following examples the DIR command is used to display the results of the RENAME command.

Changing a Filename and/or a Filename Extension

1. Insert the DOS System diskette in drive A.
2. Insert a scratch diskette in drive B.
3. With A> as the prompt, enter the following DOS command to create a scratch copy of the DOS System diskette in drive B:

   ```
   A>DISKCOPY A: B:
   ```

4. With A> as the prompt, enter the following DOS commands:

   ```
   A>DIR B:F*
   A>RENAME B:FORMAT.COM FRMT.COM
   A>DIR B:F*
   ```

   The RENAME command changes the name of a single file—in this case, from FORMAT.COM to FRMT.COM—in the directory of the diskette in the specified drive (drive B). Note that the disk drive specifier is not included as part of the new file specification.
5. With A> as the prompt, enter the following DOS commands:

   ```
   A>RENAME B:FIND.COM FIND.OLD
   A>DIR B:F*
   ```

   The RENAME command changes the filename extension of a single file—in this case, FIND.COM from .COM to .OLD—in the directory of the diskette in the specified drive (drive B).
6. Change the default drive to drive B.
7. With B> as the prompt, enter the following DOS commands:

   ```
   B>RENAME FDISK.COM FIXDISK.BAK
   B>DIR F*
   ```

   The RENAME command changes the filename and extension of a single file—in this case, from FDISK.COM to FIXDISK.BAK—in the directory of the diskette in the default drive (drive B).

Note: Wildcard characters can be used in the RENAME command to rename groups of files in the same disk directory having similar file names.

PROTECTING FILES FROM ACCIDENTAL DELETION

At some point you might accidentally delete a file from a disk. You should realize that the DEL command does not destroy the information in the specified file(s); it only marks the file name(s) in the disk's directory as a deleted file(s). Consequently, files deleted with the DEL command can be recovered through the use of special utility programs if the information has not been destroyed by writing additional information on the disk.

There are several things that you can do to help prevent the accidental deletion of file names from the directory of a disk.

- First and foremost, you should be very careful when you use the DEL or ERASE command. Double-check the file names specified in the DEL command before you press the Enter key.
- Second, a write-protect tab can be placed over the write-protect notch on the edge of the diskette jacket to protect an entire diskette. However, use of a write-protect tab prevents you from writing any additional information on this diskette.
- Third, before you use a wildcard character in a DEL command, you should use the same wildcard specification in a DIR command to verify that the files you intend to delete are the files that are included with the wildcard specification.
- Finally, the **ATTRIB** (ATTRIBute) command (new to DOS Version 3.0) allows you to selectively declare files as read-only files. Files that are declared as read-only files cannot be modified or deleted by using the DEL or ERASE command.

Changing the Read-Only File Access Attribute (ATTRIB)

1. Insert the DOS System diskette in drive A.
2. With A> as the prompt, enter the following DOS command:

   ```
   A>ATTRIB +R COMMAND.COM
   ```

   After the ATTRIB program is loaded into memory from the DOS System diskette in drive A, the +R parameter instructs the ATTRIB command to declare a single file—in this case, COMMAND.COM—on the diskette in the default drive (drive A) as a read-only file.
3. With A> as the prompt, enter the following DOS command:

   ```
   A>ATTRIB COMMAND.COM
   ```

   After the ATTRIB program is loaded into memory from the DOS System diskette in drive A, it displays the following attribute status of a single file—in this case, COMMAND.COM—on the diskette in the default drive (drive A):

   ```
   R A     A:\COMMAND.COM
   ```

   The R indicates that this file is a read-only file.

4. With A> as the prompt, enter the following DOS command:

```
A>DEL COMMAND.COM
```

Since the specified file COMMAND.COM in the DEL command is a read-only file, DEL displays the following message before returning to command level without deleting the file:

```
Access denied
```

5. With A> as the prompt, enter the following DOS command:

```
A>ATTRIB -R COMMAND.COM
```

The -R parameter instructs the ATTRIB command to remove the read-only status from the specified file COMMAND.COM on the diskette in the default drive (drive A).

Notes about the ATTRIB Command

- Since read-only files cannot be modified or deleted, data files used with application programs such as a word processor should not be given a read-only status.
- The read-only status of a group of files can be turned on or off by using wildcard characters to specify multiple file names in the ATTRIB command.
- When a read-only file is copied with the COPY or XCOPY command, the read-only status is not transferred to the target file.

6 Backing up Diskettes and Files

Making backup copies of important files and complete diskettes minimizes the amount of time and information you might lose if something goes wrong with a particular file or an entire diskette. Even though you are very careful with your diskettes, they can be misplaced or damaged by accident, and files can be inadvertently modified or deleted. The effort it takes to make these backup copies is a very wise investment of your time.

This chapter will present several ways in which you can back up diskettes and files, pointing out advantages and disadvantages of each method when appropriate. The DOS commands DISKCOPY, COPY, XCOPY, DISKCOMP, and COMP will be utilized in this chapter. Recall that the DISKCOPY command was first introduced in Chapter 2 and the COPY command was covered extensively in Chapter 5. COPY is an internal DOS command, while DISKCOPY, XCOPY, DISKCOMP, and COMP are all external DOS commands.

MAKING IDENTICAL DISKETTE COPIES (DISKCOPY)

The **DISKCOPY** command allows you to copy the entire contents of one diskette (source) onto another diskette (target). If necessary, the DISKCOPY command will automatically format the target diskette to the source diskette format. The process outlined below assumes that you are working on a computer system with two diskette drives. If you have only one diskette drive, you should refer to the section "Making Copies Using One Diskette Drive" in Chapter 2.

1. Insert the DOS System diskette in drive A.
2. With A> as the prompt, enter the following DOS command:

   ```
   A>DISKCOPY A: B:
   ```

   After the DISKCOPY program is loaded into memory from the DOS System diskette in drive A, it displays a prompt message about the source diskette and the target diskette.
3. Remove the DOS System diskette from drive A and insert your source diskette (diskette to be backed up) in drive A.
4. Insert a target diskette in drive B.

   If the target diskette is not formatted, the DISKCOPY program will format it during the copying process.
5. Press any key.

   When the copying process is complete, the following message is displayed:

   ```
   Copy another diskette (Y/N)?
   ```
6. Enter Y if you want to make another diskette copy.

   Enter N if you want to exit the DISKCOPY program.

Disadvantages of Using the DISKCOPY Command

The DISKCOPY command is an easy command to use when making backup copies of diskettes. If you want to make an identical copy of a source diskette or if the source diskette has any hidden files that you want copied, then you should use the DISKCOPY command. There are, however, some disadvantages to using the DISKCOPY command.

- If the source diskette has any bad sectors on it, the same sectors on the target diskette will be labeled as bad sectors. The DISKCOPY command might display a message similar to the following:

  ```
  Unrecoverable read error on drive A:
  Side 1, track 39

  Target diskette may be unusable
  ```

- If the target diskette contains bad sectors, the information written to these sectors might not be usable. The DISKCOPY command does not check the target diskette for bad sectors; it copies the source diskette sector by sector to the target diskette. Consequently, no message about this possible problem is ever displayed. This problem can be alleviated by first formatting the target diskette with the FORMAT command and then checking it for bad sectors with the CHKDSK command. If a diskette contains bad sectors, do not use it as the target diskette for the DISKCOPY command.
- If the source diskette contains fragmented files (Chapter 4), the file fragmentation is duplicated on the target diskette. Regular use of fragmented files will slow DOS's reading speed, since the disk drive's read/write heads will have to be moved to several disjointed locations on the disk when accessing a fragmented file.

BACKING UP FILES USING TWO DISKETTE DRIVES

This section contains alternative methods for backing up files and diskettes. If you do not need an identical copy of a diskette and if you do not want to copy any hidden files, then you should consider choosing one of the procedures outlined in this section to back up files and to make duplicate (not identical) copies of diskettes.

Backing up Files with the COPY Command

The COPY command can be used to back up individual files, groups of files, or all files specified in the directory on a disk. The following example illustrates the use of the COPY command to back up all user files on a diskette.

1. Insert your source diskette in drive A.
2. Insert a formatted target diskette in drive B.
3. With A> as the prompt, enter the following DOS command:

   ```
   A>COPY *.* B:
   ```

   The COPY command copies all user files from the diskette in the default drive (drive A) to the diskette in the specified drive (drive B).

Note: If the directory of the diskette inserted in drive B is empty, file fragmentation on the source diskette will be eliminated on the target diskette through the use of the above copying process. For a comprehensive discussion of the COPY command, you should refer to Chapter 5.

Backing up Files with the XCOPY Command (Interactive Selection)

The **XCOPY** command can be used to selectively copy files from a disk in one drive to a disk in another drive. Note that XCOPY is a new command in DOS Version 3.20.

1. Insert the DOS System diskette in drive A.
2. Insert a formatted target diskette in drive B.
3. With A> as the prompt, enter the following DOS command:

   ```
   A>XCOPY A: B: /W /P
   ```

   After the XCOPY program is loaded into memory from the DOS System diskette in drive A, the /W parameter instructs XCOPY to display the following message and to wait before it starts to copy any files:

   ```
   Press any key to begin copying file(s)
   ```

   Note: A space is not necessary before a slash (/), since a slash is interpreted by DOS as a parameter delimiter (separator).

4. Remove the DOS System diskette from drive A and insert the source diskette that contains files to be backed up in drive A.
5. Press any key.

   The /P parameter instructs XCOPY to prompt you with (Y/N)? after each file name in the directory of the source diskette in drive A before it copies that file from the diskette in drive A to the diskette in drive B.
6. If you press the Y key, the specified file is copied, and a prompt for the next file name in the directory is displayed.

   If you press the N key, the specified file is not copied, and a prompt for the next file name in the directory is displayed.

   This process should be repeated until XCOPY has prompted you with each file name in the directory of the source diskette.

Note: You can restrict the file specifications displayed by the XCOPY command to certain groups of files by using wildcard characters. For example, if you replace the command in item 3 above with the command

```
XCOPY *.DOC B:/W/P
```

you will be prompted with (Y/N)? after each file name from the directory of the diskette in the default drive (drive A) having .DOC as the filename extension.

Backing up Files with the XCOPY Command (Dated Selection)

The XCOPY command can be used to copy files from a disk in one drive to a disk in another drive on the basis of a specified date. The general format of the date parameter is /D:*mm–dd–yy*, where *mm* denotes the month (01 through 12), *dd* denotes the day (01 through 31), and *yy* denotes the year (80 through 99 or 1980 through 1999).

1. Insert the DOS System diskette in drive A.
2. Insert a formatted target diskette in drive B.
3. With A> as the prompt, enter the following DOS command:

   ```
   A>XCOPY A: B: /W /D:01-31-88
   ```

   After the XCOPY program is loaded into memory from the DOS System diskette in drive A, the /W parameter instructs XCOPY to display the following message:

   Press any key to begin copying file(s)

   Note: A space is not necessary before a slash (/) since a slash is interpreted by DOS as a parameter delimiter (separator).

4. Remove the DOS System diskette from drive A and insert the source diskette that contains files to be backed up in drive A.
5. Press any key.

   The /D:01–31–88 parameter instructs the XCOPY command to copy each source file that has a creation or modification date on or after the specified date—in this case, 01–31–88—from the source diskette in drive A to the target diskette in drive B.

Note: You can also use the date specification in an interactive selection mode. For example, if you replace the command in item 3 above with the command

```
XCOPY A: B:/W/P/D:01-31-88
```

you will be prompted with (Y/N)? after each file name from the directory of the diskette in drive A that has a creation or modification date on or after the specified date (01–31–88).

COMPARING THE CONTENTS OF TWO DISKETTES (DISKCOMP)

Suppose you have two diskettes that appear to be the same, but you want to know whether the diskettes are identical copies. The **DISKCOMP** (DISK COMPare) command allows you to compare the entire contents of two diskettes on a track-by-track basis and display any differences in the compared diskettes.

1. Insert the DOS System diskette in drive A.
2. With A> as the prompt, enter the following DOS command:

   ```
   A>DISKCOMP A: B:
   ```

   After the DISKCOMP program is loaded into memory from the DOS System diskette in drive A, it displays the following messages:

   Insert FIRST diskette in drive A:

   Insert SECOND diskette in drive B:

   Press any key when ready . . .

3. Remove the DOS System diskette from drive A and insert the first diskette in drive A.
4. Insert the second diskette in drive B.
5. Press any key.

   The DISKCOMP program displays the following message:

   Comparing 40 tracks
   9 sectors per track, 2 side(s)

   If the two diskettes are identical copies, DISKCOMP displays the messages:

   Compare OK

   Compare another diskette (Y/N)?

   If the two diskettes are not identical copies, DISKCOMP displays a message similar to the following for each track that does not compare favorably:

   Compare error on side 0, track 36

6. Enter Y and follow the prompt messages to compare two additional diskettes. That is, repeat steps 3–5.

   Enter N to exit the DISKCOMP program.

COMPARING THE CONTENTS OF FILES (COMP)

Two diskettes might not be identical copies but might contain the same file names (possibly stored in the directories of the diskettes in different orders) and identical information in the corresponding files. The **COMP** (COMPare) command allows you to compare the contents of two files or two sets of files and display any differences in the compared files.

Comparing the Contents of Two Files

1. Insert the DOS System diskette in drive A.
2. With A> as the prompt, enter the following DOS command:

   `A>COMP`

   After the COMP program is loaded into memory from the DOS System diskette in drive A, it displays the following message:

   `Enter primary file name`

3. Remove the DOS System diskette from drive A and insert the diskette in drive A that contains the files that you want to compare.
4. Respond to the prompt message given in item 2 by entering the name of the first file that you want to compare.

   COMP displays the following message:

   `Enter 2nd file name or drive id`

5. Enter the name of the second file that you want to compare.

   If the two specified files contain identical information, COMP displays the following message:

   `Files compare ok`

   If the two specified files do not contain identical information, COMP displays an appropriate message about their differences. In either case, COMP displays the following message:

   `Compare more files (Y/N)?`

6. Enter Y and follow the prompt messages to compare additional files. That is, repeat steps 3–5.

   Enter N to exit the COMP program.

Note: Files on two different disks may be compared by including the appropriate drive designator in front of the specified file name when responding to the COMP prompts. Wildcard characters can also be used with the COMP command to specify the comparison of groups of files with similar file names.

Comparing the Contents of All Files on Two Different Diskettes

1. Insert the DOS System diskette in drive A.
2. With A> as the prompt, enter the following DOS command:

   `A>COMP`

   After the COMP program is loaded into memory from the DOS System diskette in drive A, it displays the following message:

   `Enter the primary file name`

3. Remove the DOS System diskette from drive A and insert the first diskette in drive A and the second diskette in drive B.
4. Respond to the prompt message given in item 2 by entering the following file specification:

   `A:*.*`

   COMP displays the following message:

   `Enter 2nd file name or drive id`

5. Enter the following file specification:

   `B:*.*`

   The COMP program compares each file on the diskette in drive A with the file having the same file name on the diskette in drive B. After each pair of files is compared, COMP displays the following message if the files contain identical information:

   `Files compare ok`

   If two compared files do not contain identical information, COMP displays an appropriate message about their differences. After all of the specified files have been compared, the COMP program displays the following message:

   `Compare more files (Y/N)?`

6. Enter Y and follow the prompt messages to compare additional files. That is, repeat steps 3–5.

   Enter N to exit the COMP program.

7 Creating and Viewing Text Files

DOS commands can be used to create text (character, ASCII format) files and to view information in text files. In this chapter the DIR and COPY commands are used to create text files. The TYPE, MORE, and PRINT commands are used to display information in text files. DIR, COPY, and TYPE are internal DOS commands, while MORE and PRINT are external DOS commands.

CREATING A TEXT FILE WITH THE DIR COMMAND

The output redirection operator > can be used with the DIR command to create a text file that contains the directory information generated by the DIR command. This can be accomplished by following the redirection operator with a file specification.

1. Insert the DOS System diskette in drive A.
2. Insert a formatted diskette in drive B.
3. With A> as the prompt, enter the following DOS command:

   ```
   A>DIR > B:DIRFILE.TXT
   ```

   The DIR command generates the directory listing of the diskette in the default drive (drive A). Instead of the output from the DIR command being displayed on the screen, it is redirected by > to the specified file—in this case, DIRFILE.TXT—on the diskette in drive B.

CREATING A TEXT FILE WITH THE COPY COMMAND (COPY CON)

The COPY command can be used to create text files by copying information entered directly from the keyboard console (CON) to the file specified in the command. This process is a convenient way to generate short text files.

1. Insert a formatted diskette in drive A.
2. With A> as the prompt, enter the following DOS command:

   ```
   A>COPY CON A:INFO.TXT
   ```

   The COPY command instructs DOS to copy the characters entered from the keyboard console (CON) to the target file specified in the COPY command—in this case, INFO.TXT on the diskette in drive A. Since drive A is the default drive, the drive designator A: does not have to be specified in the above command.
3. Enter the desired text lines, pressing the Enter key at the end of each line. For example, the following lines may be entered:

   ```
   "This example creates a file called INFO.TXT on the
   diskette in drive A and then copies the information
   entered from the keyboard console (CON) into the
   file."
   ```

4. Enter an end-of-file marker with Ctrl-Z (hold the Ctrl key down and press the Z key); then press the Enter key.

   Entering the end-of-file marker completes the copying process for the above COPY command.

Note: The COPY CON command will be used in Chapter 9 to create batch files.

DISPLAYING INFORMATION IN A TEXT FILE (TYPE)

The **TYPE** command instructs DOS to display the contents of a specified file on the standard output device (normally the screen). Although the TYPE command can be used to display any file, only text files are displayed in a legible format. Using the TYPE command to display information in a nontext file usually produces unreadable information owing to the presence of special character codes, control characters, and escape sequences (nondisplayable characters) in the file. It might also cause strange things to happen to your personal computer. Your system might crash, your keyboard might lock up, or your screen might change characteristics. If this happens, you might have to restart (boot) your system.

1. Insert a diskette containing a text file in drive A. Assume that the file name INFO.TXT specifies a text file on this diskette.
2. With A> as the prompt, enter the following DOS command:

   ```
   A>TYPE INFO.TXT
   ```

The TYPE command instructs DOS to display the contents of the specified file—in this case, INFO.TXT on the diskette in the default drive (drive A)—on the screen.

3. Insert the DOS System diskette in drive B.
4. With A> as the prompt, enter the following DOS command:

```
A>TYPE B:COMP.COM
```

The TYPE command instructs DOS to display the contents of the specified file—in this case, COMP.COM on the diskette in drive B—on the screen. Since COMP.COM is not a text file, the information in this file is not displayed in a readable format.

DISPLAYING INFORMATION IN A TEXT FILE ONE SCREEN AT A TIME (TYPE ¦ MORE)

When you use the TYPE command to display a large text file, you notice that it cannot all be displayed in one screen image. The first part of the file scrolls off the top of the screen before it can be read. There are three ways to pause the output to the screen so that you will have time to read it. One method involves sending an interrupt message to DOS instructing it to suspend output to the screen until it receives a continue message. This is accomplished by entering Ctrl-S (hold the Ctrl key down and press the S key). Output to the screen immediately stops but will continue when any key is pressed. (Note that Ctrl-S and Ctrl-NumLock have a similar effect in this situation.) The other two methods involve the use of the **MORE** command, a command that instructs DOS to display one full screen of information at a time. The following examples illustrate the use of the MORE command to control the amount of information displayed from a text file.

1. Insert the DOS System diskette in drive A.
2. Insert a diskette containing a text file in drive B. Assume that the file name DIRFILE.TXT specifies a text file on this diskette.
3. With A> as the prompt, enter the following DOS command:

```
A>TYPE B:DIRFILE.TXT ¦ MORE
```

The TYPE command instructs DOS to read the information in the specified file—in this case, DIRFILE.TXT on the diskette in drive B. Normally, this information is displayed on the screen. However, the piping symbol ¦ instructs DOS to pipe (send) the output of the TYPE command to the MORE command as input. After the MORE program is loaded into memory from the DOS System diskette in drive A, it begins displaying the contents of the specified text file DIRFILE.TXT on the screen. When a full screen of information is displayed, the output listing pauses, and the MORE command displays the following message:

```
-- More --
```

4. Press any key.

   The contents of the file continue to be displayed on the screen, pausing each time the screen is filled with new information.

5. With A> as the prompt, enter the following DOS command:

   ```
   A>MORE < B:DIRFILE.TXT
   ```

   This command performs the same process as the command in item 3 above. After the MORE program is loaded into memory from the DOS System diskette in drive A, the contents of the specified file—in this case, DIRFILE.TXT on the diskette in drive B—are directed as input to the MORE command by <, the input redirection operator. The MORE command displays the information in the specified file one screen at a time.

PRINTING THE CONTENTS OF A TEXT FILE (PRINT)

The **PRINT** command allows you to print the contents of a text file or group of text files on your printer while you are executing other DOS commands.

1. Insert the DOS System diskette in drive A.
2. Insert a diskette containing a text file in drive B. Assume that the file name INFO.TXT specifies a text file on this diskette.
3. Ready your printer.
4. With A> as the prompt, enter the following DOS command to print the specified text file—in this case, INFO.TXT on the diskette in drive B—on your printer:

   ```
   A>PRINT B:INFO.TXT
   ```

   After the PRINT program is loaded into memory from the DOS System diskette in drive A, it displays the following message:

   Name of list device [PRN]:

5. Press the Enter key.

   The following message is displayed:

   Resident part of PRINT installed

   Note that the above two messages appear only the first time you execute the PRINT command. The following message is displayed before the information in the specified text file is sent to the printer.

   B:\INFO.TXT is currently being printed

   When the printing process is complete, the PRINT command issues a page ejection command to the printer.

6. With A> as the prompt, enter the following DOS command:

   ```
   A>PRINT B:*.TXT
   ```

   After the PRINT program is loaded into memory from the DOS System diskette in drive A, it sends from the diskette in drive B each file having the specified filename extension—in this case, .TXT—to the printer. The specification for each file sent to the printer is displayed on the screen.

DIRECTING THE CONTENTS OF A TEXT FILE TO THE PRINTER (COPY filespec PRN)

There are two disadvantages in using the PRINT command to print a text file on a printer. First, since PRINT is an external command, it must be available on a disk in a drive before it can be used. Second, the PRINT command always issues a page ejection command to the printer after each file is printed. If your text files are short, you might want more than one file printed on a page. The following two examples show how to eliminate both of these disadvantages.

1. Insert a diskette containing a text file in drive A. Assume that the file name INFO.TXT specifies a text file on the diskette.
2. Ready your printer.
3. With A> as the prompt, enter the following DOS command:

   ```
   A>COPY INFO.TXT PRN
   ```

   The COPY command instructs DOS to copy from the default drive (drive A) the contents of the specified text file—in this case, INFO.TXT—to the printer that is denoted by PRN.
4. With A> as the prompt, enter the following DOS command:

   ```
   A>TYPE INFO.TXT > PRN
   ```

   The output redirection operator > instructs DOS to direct the output of the TYPE command—in this case, the information in the specified file INFO.TXT on the diskette in drive A—to the printer that is denoted by PRN.

8 Using a Fixed Disk

This chapter is devoted primarily to DOS commands that are used to help manage information on a fixed disk. You should note that each command presented in this chapter can also be used on a diskette drive. Therefore, even if you do not have a personal computer with a fixed disk, you can perform the commands presented in this chapter on a diskette drive.

The MKDIR (MD), CHDIR (CD), and RMDIR (RD) commands are used to help you manage multiple directories on a disk. The PROMPT, TREE, and PATH commands are used to assist you in working with a disk that has several directories. Finally, the BACKUP and RESTORE commands are used to back up and restore files on a disk. MKDIR, CHDIR, RMDIR, PROMPT, and PATH are all internal DOS commands, while TREE, BACKUP, and RESTORE are external DOS commands.

Note: The material presented in this chapter assumes that DOS has been installed on your fixed disk in drive C and that all files from the DOS System diskette and the DOS Supplemental Programs diskette have been copied onto the fixed disk. If this is not the case, refer to the section "Preparing a Fixed Disk for Use with DOS" in Chapter 3.

MANAGING DISK FILES

When you first begin to use a personal computer, you probably have three or four diskettes that you regularly use: a DOS System diskette, one or two diskettes containing application programs such as word processing programs, and a data diskette. Initially, you have one diskette to hold all of your data files. As the number of files grows, you realize that managing a large number of unrelated files on one data diskette is not a good idea. At this point you decide to separate your data files into similar categories and put each category of files onto a separate diskette containing an appropriate label. The same thing occurs with application programs. You separate different application programs by putting them on different diskettes. Through the use of multiple diskettes you are better able to manage your computer application programs and their associated data files.

Managing information on a fixed disk is similar to managing information in an office file cabinet. Suppose you store letters, memorandums, reports, and other items in a file cabinet without using any labeled file folders and without using any topical organization of the information in the file cabinet. The lack of any file cabinet organization is fine until you try to locate a particular piece of information. The more information you have in an unorganized file cabinet, the more trouble you will have in trying to locate any particular item in the cabinet. Consequently, you put labels on file folders and separate groups of file folders according to certain common characteristics so that information can be retrieved in a timely manner. These same ideas carry over to storing files of information on a fixed disk. You must organize your computer files in a manner that allows you to effectively use a fixed disk. This is accomplished through the use of multiple directories.

TYPES OF DIRECTORIES

Recall from Chapter 4 that a directory is a table of contents or an index that DOS maintains about information that is stored on a disk. The directory of a disk contains an entry for each file on the disk that consists of the filename, the filename extension, the file size in bytes, the date and time the file was created or last updated, and the location of the beginning of the file data on the disk.

Root Directory

A directory is created by DOS each time the FORMAT command is used to format a disk. This directory is called the **main (root) directory** of a disk. The main directory is commonly called the root directory because a multilevel directory structure, called a **tree structure**, can grow from it.

Subdirectories

To make your computer filing system more flexible, DOS allows you to create additional directories on a disk, called **subdirectories**. Subdirectories allow you to divide a disk into separate storage areas that can be used like separate disks. A subdirectory is a special file that contains directory entries. These entries have the same form as the entries in the root directory. Since a subdirectory is a directory, the terms subdirectory and directory may be used interchangeably in some places. This is similar to the idea that all members of your family are human beings, but at the same time you are also family members with special names and titles.

Naming Subdirectories

Subdirectory names follow the same format as file names, consisting of one to eight characters followed by an optional extension consisting of a period and one to three characters. All valid characters for file names are also valid for subdirectory names. Normally subdirectory names are short and do not include extensions; this makes them convenient to use.

Current Directory

The **current directory** associated with a disk is the directory that you are currently working in or the directory that you were working in on another drive. DOS keeps track of the current directory in the same way that it keeps track of the current (default) disk drive. When the system is booted, the current drive is the drive containing the disk from which the DOS system programs were loaded into memory, and the current directory is the root directory of the disk in this drive. The terminology **current directory** is used to denote the current directory of the disk in the default drive. The terminology **current directory of a drive** is used to denote the current directory of the disk in that drive.

Directory Path

When DOS is attempting to locate a file and no particular directory is specified, DOS looks for the file only in the current directory. If the file is in another directory, DOS must be given directions on how to access that directory. A **directory path** or **path** is the route you must follow to trace your way from the disk's main or root directory to a particular place in the directory structure. The description of a path is called the **directory path name**, **path name**, or **path specification**.

Consider the multilevel directory structure given in Fig. 8.1. Note that this tree structure grows out of the root directory. The root directory contains three subdirectories SD–1, SD–2, and SD–3. Directory SD–1 contains one subdirectory (SD–11); directory SD–2 contains two subdirectories (SD–21 and SD–22); and directory SD–3 contains no subdirectories.

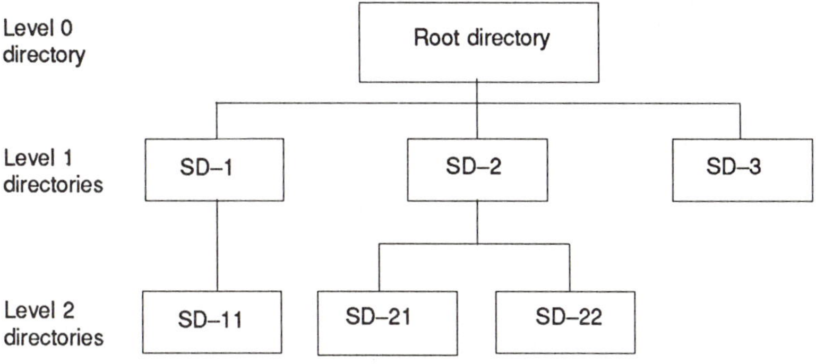

Figure 8.1 Multilevel Directory Structure

Suppose that you want to access a file in subdirectory SD–21. You get to this directory through the following path of directories: root directory to subdirectory SD–2 to subdirectory SD–21. The path name (specification) for this path is \SD-2\SD–21. In this specification the initial backslash (\) instructs DOS to start the path at the root directory, while the second backslash is used as a directory name delimiter.

Suppose that the file name EXAMPLE.DOC is contained in subdirectory SD-22. The following specification contains the directory path name and the file name and denotes the complete specification for the file EXAMPLE.DOC:

```
\SD-2\SD-22\EXAMPLE.DOC
```

Note that the specification begins with the root directory and gets to the file EXAMPLE.DOC in subdirectory SD–22 by going through subdirectory SD–2.

Path Name Notation

A path name consisting of only the **backslash (\)** specifies the root directory. A path name beginning with a backslash (\) specifies that the path starts in the root directory. The backslash (\) is also used as a delimiter between two directory names or between a directory name and a file name.

Directory Structure Terminology

If U and V are subdirectories of a directory T, then U and V are **offspring directories** of T, T is called the **parent directory** for U and V, and U and V are **sibling directories**. Using the notation of Fig. 8.1, subdirectories SD–21 and SD–22 are siblings and have SD–2 as their parent directory. Subdirectory SD–11 is an offspring of directory SD–1.

SUBDIRECTORY COMMANDS

You are now ready to create and use a directory structure similar to the one given in Fig. 8.1. Since subdirectories are special types of files, special DOS commands must be used to create (MKDIR, MD), change (CHDIR, CD), and remove (RMDIR, RD) a subdirectory.

Note: If your personal computer contains a fixed disk, C> is the DOS prompt for this drive. If you do not have a fixed disk on your personal computer, insert a bootable diskette in drive A that contains the three external DOS commands CHKDSK, FORMAT, and TREE, and use drive A instead of drive C to practice the DOS commands covered in the next several sections.

CREATING (MAKING) SUBDIRECTORIES (MKDIR, MD)

The **MKDIR** (MaKe DIRectory) command instructs DOS to create a subdirectory with the directory path and name being specified in the command. **MD** is an abbreviation of the MKDIR command. The MKDIR command can be used to create the directory structure of Fig. 8.1 by following the process outlined below.

Creating Subdirectories in the Root Directory (First Level)

The examples in this section illustrate the creation of subdirectories in the root directory. In particular, the level 1 directories SD–1, SD–2, and SD–3 of the directory structure in Fig. 8.1 are created in this section. Assume that the current directory of the fixed disk in drive C is the root directory.

1. With C> as the prompt, enter the following DOS commands:

   ```
   C>MKDIR SD-1
   C>MKDIR SD-2
   C>MD SD-3
   C>DIR
   ```

   The MKDIR and MD commands instruct DOS to create the specified subdirectories—in this case, SD–1, SD–2, and SD–3—in the root directory of the fixed disk in drive C. The DIR command displays all the file entries in the root directory of the fixed disk, including the three newly created subdirectories.

2. With C> as the prompt, enter the following DOS command to display the subdirectory entries:

   ```
   C>DIR SD-*
   ```

   The DIR command instructs DOS to display all entries in the current directory of the default drive (drive C) having SD– as their first three characters. DOS displays information similar to the following:

   ```
    Volume in drive C is FIXED-DISK
    Directory of  C:\

   SD-1          <DIR>        1-31-88   10:46p
   SD-2          <DIR>        1-31-88   10:46p
   SD-3          <DIR>        1-31-88   10:46p
           3 File(s)   31139840 bytes free
   ```

   Note that `C:\` in the second line indicates that the three listed directories are subdirectories of the root directory in drive C. Also note that `<DIR>` specifies that the listed names are directory names.

3. With C> as the prompt, enter the following DOS command:

   ```
   C>DIR SD-1
   ```

   The DIR command instructs DOS to display the contents of the specified directory—in this case, subdirectory SD–1 on the disk in the default drive (drive C). DOS displays information similar to the following:

```
Volume in drive C is FIXED-DISK
Directory of  C:\SD-1

.              <DIR>        1-31-88   10:46p
..             <DIR>        1-31-88   10:46p
        2 File(s)   31139840 bytes free
```

Note that the newly created directory SD–1 contains two special directory entries. The **single period entry** (.) in a subdirectory represents the current directory. The **double period entry** (..) in a subdirectory represents the parent directory. All directories except the root directory will always contain these two entries.

Creating Second-Level Subdirectories from the Root Directory

The examples in this section illustrate the creation of second-level subdirectories from the root directory. In particular, the level 2 directories SD–11, SD–21, and SD–22 of the directory structure in Fig. 8.1 are created in this section. Assume that the current directory of the fixed disk in drive C is the root directory.

1. With C> as the prompt, enter the following DOS command:

   ```
   C>MD \SD-1\SD-11
   ```

   The MD command (abbreviated MKDIR command) instructs DOS to create the specified subdirectory—in this case, subdirectory SD–11 in directory SD–1 on the disk in the default drive (drive C). Note that \SD–1 in the above command specifies a directory path. Also note that the leading backslash in the path specification of the above command is not necessary, since the current directory is the root directory and since SD–1 is a subdirectory of the root directory.

2. With C> as the prompt, enter the following DOS command:

   ```
   C>DIR SD-1
   ```

   The DIR command instructs DOS to display the contents of the specified directory—in this case, subdirectory SD–1 on the disk in the default drive (drive C). DOS displays information similar to the following:

   ```
   Volume in drive C is FIXED-DISK
   Directory of  C:\SD-1

   .              <DIR>        1-31-88   10:46p
   ..             <DIR>        1-31-88   10:46p
   SD-11          <DIR>        1-31-88   10:50p
           3 File(s)   31137792 bytes free
   ```

   The DIR command knows that SD–1 is a directory name because of the *<DIR>* designator for SD–1 in the root directory.

3. With C> as the prompt, enter the following DOS commands:

```
C>MD SD-2\SD-21
C>MD SD-2\SD-22
C>DIR SD-2
```

The MD commands instruct DOS to create the specified subdirectories—in this case, subdirectories SD–21 and SD–22 in directory SD–2 on the disk in the default drive (drive C). The DIR command instructs DOS to display the contents of directory SD–2. Note that the path specification (SD–2) in each of the MD commands does not begin with a backslash, since the current directory is the root directory and since SD–2 is a subdirectory of the root directory.

Note: The creation of the multilevel directory structure given in Fig. 8.1 is now complete.

4. With C> as the prompt, enter the following DOS command:

```
C>CHKDSK
```

After the CHKDSK program is loaded into memory from the root directory of the fixed disk, it displays a status report for the fixed disk in drive C that includes a statement similar to the following:

```
    12288 bytes in 6 directories
```

Note that you created six directories with the MD command.

Note: All of the subdirectories in Fig. 8.1 have unique names. You can create two or more subdirectories with the same name as long as they have different path specifications. For example, MD \SD–1\SUBDIR and MD \SD–3\SUBDIR create two different subdirectories with the name SUBDIR. One is a subdirectory of SD–1 with path specification \SD–1\SUBDIR and the other is a subdirectory of SD–3 with path specification \SD–3\SUBDIR.

CHANGING THE CURRENT DIRECTORY (CHDIR, CD)

The material in this section shows you how to declare any directory on a disk as the current directory. The **CHDIR** (CHange DIRectory) command instructs DOS to change the current directory of a disk to the directory specified in the command. This command can also be used to display the current directory. **CD** is an abbreviation of the CHDIR command. Remember that a leading backslash (\) in a path name tells DOS to begin the path at the root directory.

Changing the Current Directory to a Subdirectory

Assume that the directory structure in Fig. 8.1 is on the fixed disk in drive C and that the current directory of the fixed disk is the root directory. The DIR command is used in some of the following examples to display the current directory name and directory entries.

1. With C> as the prompt, enter the following DOS commands:

```
C>CHDIR \SD-2
C>DIR
```

   The CHDIR command instructs DOS to change the current directory of the disk in the default drive (drive C) to the specified directory—in this case, subdirectory SD–2. Since the root directory was the current directory, the leading backslash in the path specification is not necessary. Note that the DIR command lists the current directory specification as C:\SD–2.

2. With C> as the prompt, enter the following DOS commands:

```
C>CD SD-21
C>DIR
```

   The CD command instructs DOS to change the current directory of the disk in the default drive (drive C) to the specified directory—in this case, subdirectory SD–21, a subdirectory of SD–2. Note that the DIR command lists the current directory specification as C:\SD–2\SD–21.

3. With C> as the prompt, enter the following DOS command:

```
C>CD SD-22
```

   The CD command displays the following message:

   Invalid directory

   This message is displayed because SD–22 is not a subdirectory of the current directory SD–21.

4. With C> as the prompt, enter the following DOS command to display the path specification for the current directory of the disk in the default drive (drive C):

```
C>CD
```

   The CD command displays the following:

   C:\SD-2\SD-21

   This is the path specification for the current directory. The CD command can be used without any parameters to display the path specification for the current directory of the disk in the default drive.

Changing the Current Directory to the Parent Directory

Assume that the directory structure in Fig. 8.1 is on the fixed disk in drive C and that the current directory of the fixed disk is subdirectory SD–21.

1. With C> as the prompt, enter the following DOS command:

```
C>CD ..
```

   The CD command instructs DOS to change the current directory of the disk in the default drive (drive C) to its parent directory. Recall that the double period (..) denotes the parent directory. Since subdirectory SD–2 is the parent directory for SD–21, the new current directory is SD–2.

2. With C> as the prompt, enter the following DOS command to display the path specification for the current directory of the disk in the default drive (drive C):

   ```
   C>CD
   ```

   The CD command displays the following directory path specification:

   ```
   C:\CD-2
   ```

Changing the Current Directory to the Root Directory

Assume that the directory structure in Fig. 8.1 is on the fixed disk in drive C and that the current directory of the fixed disk is subdirectory SD–22.

1. With C> as the prompt, enter the following DOS command:

   ```
   C>CD \
   ```

   The CD command instructs DOS to change the current directory of the disk in the default drive (drive C) to the root directory.

Changing the Current Directory with a Path from the Root Directory

Assume that the directory structure of Fig. 8.1 is on the fixed disk in drive C. Notice that the path specified in each CD command begins in the root directory of the fixed disk, since the first character of the path specification is a backslash.

1. With C> as the prompt, enter the following DOS command:

   ```
   C>CD \SD-2\SD-22
   ```

   The CD command instructs DOS to change the current directory of the disk in the default drive (drive C) to the specified directory—in this case, subdirectory SD–22.

2. With C> as the prompt, enter the following DOS command:

   ```
   C>DIR ..
   ```

   The DIR command instructs DOS to display all entries in the parent directory of the current directory.

3. With C> as the prompt, enter the following DOS command:

   ```
   C>CD \SD-1\SD-11
   ```

   The CD command instructs DOS to change the current directory of the disk in the default drive (drive C) to the specified directory—in this case, subdirectory SD–11.

Changing the Current Directory with a Path from the Current Directory

Assume that the directory structure of Fig. 8.1 is on the fixed disk in drive C and that the current directory of the fixed disk is the subdirectory SD–21.

1. With C> as the prompt, enter the following DOS command:

```
C>CD ..\SD-22
```

The CD command instructs DOS to change the current directory of the disk in the default drive (drive C) to the specified directory. In this case the path specified in the above command is the parent directory of SD–21 (which is subdirectory SD–2) to subdirectory SD–22. Consequently, the new current directory of the fixed disk is subdirectory SD–22. This example shows you that a path can be specified in relation to the current directory, which may be different than the root directory.

Changing the Current Directory of Another Disk Drive

Assume that the directory structure of Fig. 8.1 is on the fixed disk in drive C.

1. With A> as the prompt, enter the following DOS commands:

```
A>CD C:\CD-2\CD-21
A>CD C:
```

The first CD command instructs DOS to change the current directory of the fixed disk in drive C to subdirectory SD–21. The second CD command instructs DOS to display the current directory specification for the disk in drive C.

2. With A> as the prompt, enter the following DOS command:

```
A>DIR C:
```

The DIR command instructs DOS to display the entries of the current directory of the fixed disk in drive C, which in this case is subdirectory SD–21.

3. Change the default drive to drive C.
4. With C> as the prompt, enter the following DOS command:

```
C>DIR
```

Note that the current directory of the fixed disk in drive C is still subdirectory SD–21. When you change the default disk drive, the current directory is not automatically set to the root directory. The current directory associated with a disk drive remains unchanged unless you change it with the CD command or change it to the root directory by rebooting the system.

Notes about Changing Directories

- Recall from the presentation of the MKDIR (MD) command that all subdirectories in Fig. 8.1 were created by specifying a path that began in the root directory. The CHDIR (CD) command allows you to change directories so that you can create subdirectories of the current directory. For example, instead of using the commands MD \SD–2\SD–21 and MD \SD–2\SD–22 to create subdirectories SD–21 and SD–22, you can change the current directory to subdirectory SD–2 with command CD \SD–2, and then use the commands MD SD–21 and MD SD–22 to create the two subdirectories.

- Recall that the information displayed by the DIR and CD commands can be redirected to the printer (PRN) by using >, the output redirection operator.

AUTOMATICALLY DISPLAYING THE CURRENT DIRECTORY NAME WITH PROMPT

Recall from the previous sections that the DIR and CD commands were used regularly to display the current directory specification. When you use a disk that has several subdirectories, you need a convenient way to keep track of the current directory. The **PROMPT** command allows you to change the normal DOS prompt to a customized DOS prompt.

Assume that the directory structure of Fig. 8.1 is on the fixed disk in drive C and that the current directory of the fixed disk is the root directory.

1. With C> as the prompt, enter the following DOS command:

   ```
   C>PROMPT $P$G
   ```

   The PROMPT command instructs DOS to change the DOS prompt to the character string specified by PG. $P specifies that the first part of the new prompt will consist of the current directory specification. $G specifies that > will be the last character in the new prompt.
2. With C:\> as the prompt, enter the following DOS command:

   ```
   C:\>CD SD-1\SD-11
   ```

   The CD command instructs DOS to change the current directory of the fixed disk in drive C to subdirectory SD–11. DOS responds with the following prompt:

   ```
   C:\SD-1\SD-11>
   ```
3. Insert a formatted disk in drive A.
4. Change the default drive to drive A.
5. With A:\> as the prompt, enter the following DOS command:

   ```
   A:\>CD C:..
   ```

   The CD command instructs DOS to change the current directory of the fixed disk in drive C to its parent directory—in this case, subdirectory SD–1.
6. Change the default drive to drive C and notice the new prompt.
7. With C:\SD–1> as the prompt, enter the following DOS command:

   ```
   C:\SD-1>PROMPT
   ```

   When the PROMPT command is used without any parameters, it instructs DOS to reset its prompt to the normal DOS prompt.

COPYING FILES BETWEEN DIFFERENT DIRECTORIES

Once you know how to specify paths to different directories, you can use the COPY and XCOPY commands to copy files from one directory to another directory in the same way that you copy files between diskettes.

Note: Recall from the beginning of this chapter that the assumption was made that all files on the DOS System diskette and the DOS Supplemental Programs diskette are in the root directory of the fixed disk in drive C.

Copying Files from the Root Directory to a Subdirectory

Assume that the directory structure of Fig. 8.1 is on the fixed disk in drive C and that the current directory of the fixed disk is the root directory.

1. With C> as the prompt, enter the following DOS command:

   ```
   C>COPY CHKDSK.COM SD-1
   ```

   The COPY command instructs DOS to copy the specified file CHKDSK.COM from the root directory (source directory) of the fixed disk to the specified subdirectory SD–1 (target directory) on the fixed disk using the same file name.
2. With C> as the prompt, enter the following DOS command:

   ```
   C>COPY FORMAT.COM SD-1\FRMT.*
   ```

   The COPY command instructs DOS to copy the specified file FORMAT.COM from the root directory of the fixed disk to the specified subdirectory SD–1 using FRMT.COM as the target file name.
3. With C> as the prompt, enter the following DOS command:

   ```
   C>DIR SD-1
   ```

   The DIR command instructs DOS to display the contents of subdirectory SD–1.
4. With C> as the prompt, enter the following DOS commands:

   ```
   C>DIR S*.*
   C>COPY S*.* SD-3
   C>DIR SD-3
   ```

   The COPY command instructs DOS to copy all files in the root directory of the disk in the default drive (drive C) having S as the first character in their file names to subdirectory SD–3 using the same file names. Note that the subdirectory entries SD–1, SD–2, and SD–3 are displayed by the first DIR command but are not copied by the COPY command. The second DIR command displays all entries in subdirectory SD–3.

Copying Files from One Subdirectory to Another Subdirectory

Assume that the directory structure of Fig. 8.1 is on the fixed disk in drive C and that the current directory of the fixed disk is the root directory.

1. With C> as the prompt, enter the following DOS commands:

   ```
   C>COPY SD-1\FRMT.COM SD-2\FORMAT.COM
   C>DIR SD-2
   ```

   The COPY command instructs DOS to copy the specified file FRMT.COM from subdirectory SD–1 on the disk in the default drive (drive C) to the specified subdirectory SD–2 on the disk in the default drive (drive C) using FORMAT.COM as the target file name.

2. With C> as the prompt, enter the following DOS command:

   ```
   C>COPY SD-3 SD-2\SD-22
   ```

   The COPY command instructs DOS to copy all files from the specified source directory—in this case, subdirectory SD–3 on the disk in the default drive (drive C)—to the specified target directory—in this case, subdirectory SD–22 on the disk in the default drive (drive C)—using the same file names.

DISPLAYING INFORMATION IN A DIRECTORY STRUCTURE

Using the DIR command to display the contents of individual directories does not give you a complete picture of the directory structure of a disk. The **TREE** command allows you to display the directory structure of the disk. Both the TREE and CHKDSK commands allow you to list the contents of each directory in the structure.

Displaying the Directory Structure of a Disk (TREE)

Assume that the directory structure of Fig. 8.1 is on the fixed disk in drive C and that the current directory of the fixed disk is the root directory.

1. With C> as the prompt, enter the following DOS command:

   ```
   C>TREE
   ```

   After the TREE program is loaded into memory from the root directory of the fixed disk, it instructs DOS to display each directory path on the fixed disk, and for each displayed path it lists the subdirectories with that path. The following information is a segment of what the above command displays:

   ```
   Path:  \SD-2

   Sub-directories:  SD-21
                     SD-22
   ```

Displaying Specifications for Subdirectory and File Names (TREE /F, CHKDSK /V)

Assume that the directory structure of Fig. 8.1 is on the fixed disk in drive C and that the current directory of the fixed disk is the root directory.

1. With C> as the prompt, enter the following DOS command:

   ```
   C>TREE /F
   ```

   After the TREE program is loaded into memory from the root directory of the fixed disk, the /F parameter instructs TREE to display all file and directory names that are in the root directory and each subdirectory of the fixed disk. The following information is a segment of what the above command displays:

   ```
   Path:    \SD-1

   Sub-directories:  SD-11
   Files:            CHKDSK   .COM
                     FRMT     .COM
   ```

   The CHKDSK command can also be used to display the path specification for each directory and the file specifications for all entries in each directory on a disk.

2. With C> as the prompt, enter the following DOS command:

   ```
   C>CHKDSK /V
   ```

   After the CHKDSK program is loaded into memory from the root directory of the fixed disk, the /V parameter instructs CHKDSK to display a list of all directory and file entries on the disk in the default drive (drive C).

Printing Specifications for Subdirectory and File Names (TREE /F > PRN, CHKDSK /V > PRN)

Assume that the directory structure of Fig. 8.1 is on the fixed disk in drive C and that the current directory of the fixed disk is the root directory. The following two examples illustrate how to send the output from the TREE and CHKDSK commands to the printer.

1. Ready your printer.
2. With C> as the prompt, enter the following DOS command:

   ```
   C>TREE /F > PRN
   ```

   After the TREE program is loaded into memory from the root directory of the fixed disk, the /F parameter instructs TREE to generate a list of all subdirectory and file names that are in the root directory and each subdirectory of the disk in the default drive (drive C). This output list from the TREE command is directed to the printer (PRN) by >, the output redirection operator.
3. With C> as the prompt, enter the following DOS command:

   ```
   C>CHKDSK /V > PRN
   ```

   After the CHKDSK program is loaded into memory from the root directory of the fixed disk, the /V parameter instructs CHKDSK to generate a list of all subdirectory and file names that are on the disk in the default drive (drive C). This output list from the CHKDSK command is directed to the printer (PRN) by >, the output redirection operator.

SETTING AN EXTENDED SEARCH PATH FOR DOS TO LOCATE COMMANDS (PATH)

Recall that an external DOS command must be loaded into memory from a disk before it can be executed. If such a command is entered and if no path specification precedes the command name, DOS searches the current directory to find the command. If the command is not in the current directory, DOS displays the message *Bad command or file name*. The **PATH** command allows you to extend the **search path** that DOS uses to locate an external DOS command.

Assume that the directory structure of Fig. 8.1 is on the fixed disk in drive C and that the current directory of the fixed disk is the root directory. The following examples illustrate how DOS searches only the current directory and directories specified in the PATH command to locate external DOS commands. The CHKDSK command is used as a sample external DOS command in the following examples. The information presented applies to any external DOS command.

1. With C> as the prompt, enter the following DOS command:

   ```
   C>PATH
   ```

   The PATH command displays the following message:

   ```
   No Path
   ```

   This means that DOS will search only the current directory for external DOS commands.

2. With C> as the prompt, enter the following DOS command:

   ```
   C>CHKDSK
   ```

   DOS searches for the CHKDSK program in the current directory—in this case, the root directory of the disk in the default drive (drive C). Since the CHKDSK program is located in the current directory, it is loaded into memory and executed.

3. With C> as the prompt, enter the following DOS commands:

   ```
   C>CD SD-3
   C>CHKDSK
   ```

   The CD command changes the current directory of the disk in the default drive (drive C) to subdirectory SD–3. DOS searches the current directory—in this case, subdirectory SD–3—to find the CHKDSK program. Since CHKDSK is not in subdirectory SD–3, DOS displays the following message:

   ```
   Bad command or file name
   ```

4. With C> as the prompt, enter the following DOS command:

   ```
   C>\CHKDSK
   ```

   The leading backslash instructs DOS to look in the root directory of the fixed disk for the CHKDSK program. The PATH command can be used to automatically tell DOS to search a directory (or directories) if it does not find the command in the current directory.

5. With C> as the prompt, enter the following DOS commands:

   ```
   C>PATH \
   C>PATH
   ```

   The first PATH command sets the extended search path to the root directory of the default drive. The second PATH command instructs DOS to display the search path you set with the last PATH command. The following message is displayed:

   ```
   PATH=\
   ```

6. With C> as the prompt, enter the following DOS command:

   ```
   C>CHKDSK
   ```

   DOS first searches for the CHKDSK program in the current directory of the disk in the default drive (drive C)—in this case, subdirectory SD–3. Since CHKDSK is not found in the current directory, DOS then determines that the root directory of the disk in the default drive is specified as an extended search path, and this is where DOS finds the CHKDSK program.

7. Insert a blank formatted diskette in drive A.
8. Change the default drive to drive A.
9. With A> as the prompt, enter the following DOS command:

   ```
   A>CHKDSK
   ```

   DOS searches the current directory of the disk in the default drive (drive A) and then the root directory of the disk in the default drive (drive A) for the CHKDSK program. DOS cannot find the CHKDSK program on the diskette in drive A, so it displays the following message:

   ```
   Bad command or file name
   ```

   Since the DOS commands are in the root directory of the fixed disk in drive C, the search path must specify more than the root directory of the disk in the default drive.

10. With A> as the prompt, enter the following DOS command:

    ```
    A>PATH C:\
    ```

    The PATH command sets the extended search path to the root directory of the fixed disk in drive C.

11. With A> as the prompt, enter the following DOS command:

    ```
    A>CHKDSK
    ```

DOS uses the extended search path—in this case, the root directory of the fixed disk in drive C—to locate and execute the CHKDSK program.

12. With A> as the prompt, enter the following DOS command:

    ```
    A>PATH;
    ```

    When the PATH command is followed by only a semicolon (;), the search path is reset to no path.

Notes about Setting an Extended Search Path for DOS

- When you boot your system, the default search path is set to null (no path).
- When an extended search path is set by the PATH command, DOS uses the extended search path to search for external commands and batch files (files having an extension of .COM, .EXE, or .BAT) that were not found while searching the current directory.

DELETING (REMOVING) SUBDIRECTORIES (RMDIR, RD)

Now that you have learned how to create and work with subdirectories, you need to know how to delete (remove) subdirectories from your directory structure. The **RMDIR** (ReMove DIRectory) command instructs DOS to remove (delete) a subdirectory entry from its parent directory. **RD** is an abbreviation of the RMDIR command. A subdirectory must be empty (except for the period (.) and double period (..) entries) before it can be removed from its parent directory. Also note that you cannot remove the current directory or the root directory of a disk.

Assume that the directory structure of Fig. 8.1 is on the fixed disk in drive C and that the current directory of the fixed disk is the root directory. The following examples illustrate how to use the RMDIR (RD) command by using it to remove (delete) the entire directory structure of Fig. 8.1 from your fixed disk.

1. With C> as the prompt, enter the following DOS commands:

    ```
    C>DIR SD-1
    C>DIR SD-1\SD-11
    C>RMDIR SD-1\SD-11
    C>DIR SD-1
    ```

    The first DIR command shows you that SD–11 is a subdirectory of directory SD–1. The second DIR command shows you that subdirectory SD–11 contains no entries except the current directory (.) and parent directory (..) entries. The RMDIR command instructs DOS to remove the subdirectory entry SD–11 from its parent directory SD–1. The final DIR command shows you that subdirectory SD–11 was removed from directory SD–1.

2. With C> as the prompt, enter the following DOS command:

    ```
    C>RD SD-1
    ```

The RD command displays the following message:

```
Invalid path, not directory,
or directory not empty
```

Recall that a directory must be empty before it can be removed.

3. With C> as the prompt, enter the following DOS commands:

```
C>DEL SD-1
C>RD SD-1
```

The DEL command instructs DOS to delete all files from subdirectory SD–1 on the disk in the default drive (drive C). The RD command instructs DOS to remove the subdirectory entry SD–1 from the root directory.

4. With C> as the prompt, enter the following DOS commands:

```
C>CD SD-2
C>RD SD-21
```

The CD command changes the current directory of the disk in the default drive (drive C) to subdirectory SD–2. The RD command instructs DOS to remove the subdirectory entry SD–21 from its parent directory SD–2.

5. With C> as the prompt, enter the following DOS commands:

```
C>DEL SD-22
C>RD SD-22
```

The DEL command instructs DOS to delete all files from subdirectory SD–22 on the disk in the default drive (drive C). The RD command instructs DOS to remove the subdirectory entry SD–22 from its parent directory SD–2.

6. With C> as the prompt, enter the following DOS commands:

```
C>CD ..
C>DEL SD-2
C>RD SD-2
```

The CD command changes the current directory of the default drive (drive C) to the parent directory—in this case, the root directory. The DEL command instructs DOS to delete all files from subdirectory SD–2. The RD command instructs DOS to remove the subdirectory entry SD–2 from its parent directory—in this case, the root directory.

7. With C> as the prompt, enter the following DOS commands:

```
C>DEL SD-3
C>RD SD-3
```

The DEL command instructs DOS to delete all files from subdirectory SD–3. The RD command instructs DOS to remove the subdirectory entry SD–3 from its parent directory—in this case, the root directory.

Note: The directory structure in Fig. 8.1 on the fixed disk in drive C should now be deleted, and your disk should be back to the original structure that it had when you began this chapter.

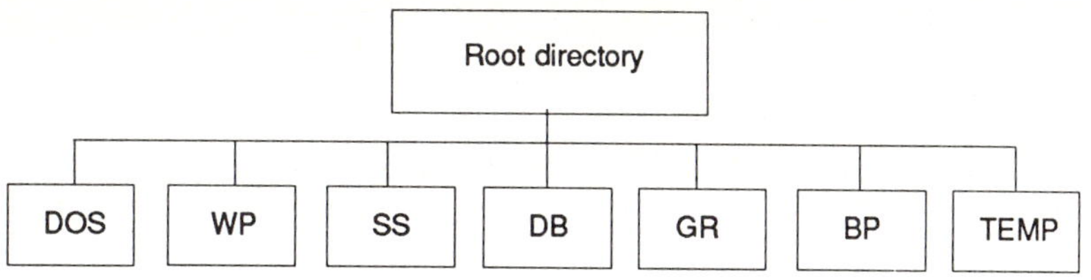

Figure 8.2 Application Directory Structure

CUSTOMIZING YOUR FIXED DISK

This section uses material presented in this chapter to help you customize your fixed disk. Subdirectories will be used to divide your fixed disk into several application areas. The root directory of your fixed disk will contain COMMAND.COM (required to be able to boot from the fixed disk), batch files (see Chapter 9), subdirectories for major application programs, and a few special files. For this section, assume that the following application areas are being used: word processing (WP), spreadsheet (SS), data base (DB), graphics (GR), and BASIC programming (BP). Figure 8.2 outlines the directory structure that will be created on the fixed disk. Note that abbreviations are used for subdirectory names to minimize key strokes when entering commands that involve path specifications. The subdirectory DOS will be used for the DOS programs. The subdirectory TEMP will allow you to have a directory to use like a scratch diskette.

WARNING: The following steps delete all nondirectory file entries in the root directory of your fixed disk in drive C. If you do not want to delete files from the root directory of your fixed disk, skip Steps 2 and 3.

1. Insert the DOS System diskette in drive A.
2. With A> as the prompt, enter the following DOS commands:

   ```
   A>CD C:\
   A>DEL C:*.*
   ```

3. Enter Y after the prompt message, `Are you sure (Y/N)?`, appears on your screen.
4. With A> as the prompt, enter the following DOS commands:

   ```
   A>COPY COMMAND.COM C:
   A>DIR C:
   A>CHKDSK C:
   ```

   The COPY command copies the specified file COMMAND.COM from the DOS System diskette in drive A to the root directory of the fixed disk. The

DIR and CHKDSK commands are used to display the current status of the fixed disk.

5. Change the default drive to drive C.
6. With C> as the prompt, enter the following DOS commands:

```
C>MD DOS
C>MD WP
C>MD SS
C>MD DB
C>MD GR
C>MD BP
C>MD TEMP
C>DIR
```

   The MD command is used to create seven subdirectories of the root directory on the fixed disk in drive C.

7. With C> as the prompt, enter the following DOS command:

```
C>CD DOS
C>COPY A:*.*
```

   The files on the DOS System diskette in drive A are copied to subdirectory DOS on the fixed disk.

8. Remove the DOS System diskette from drive A and insert the DOS Supplemental Programs diskette in drive A.
9. With C> as the prompt, enter the following DOS command:

```
C>COPY A:*.*
```

   The files on the DOS Supplemental Programs diskette in drive A are copied to subdirectory DOS on the fixed disk.

10. With C> as the prompt, enter the following DOS commands:

```
C>CD \
C>COPY DOS\BAS*.* BP
C>COPY DOS\*.BAS BP
C>DEL DOS\BAS*.*
C>DEL DOS\*.BAS
```

   After the current directory of the default drive (drive C) is changed to the route directory, the COPY commands copy all of the BASIC program files in subdirectory DOS into subdirectory BP. The BASIC program files are then deleted from subdirectory DOS.

11. Use the COPY command to copy your application programs from diskettes to the appropriate subdirectory.

Note: Each time you want to run a particular application, use the CD command to set the current directory for that application. Chapter 9 will show you how to automate this process.

Formatting a Diskette from a Fixed Disk

Once the DOS programs have been copied to your fixed disk, they may be used to perform tasks for you, such as formatting a diskette. Assume that the directory structure of Fig. 8.2 is on the fixed disk in drive C and that the current directory of the fixed disk is the root directory. Also assume that the DOS programs have been copied to subdirectory DOS on the fixed disk.

1. Insert a blank diskette to be formatted in drive A.
2. With C> as the prompt, enter the following DOS command:

   ```
   C>DOS\FORMAT A:
   ```

   The path (DOS) specified before the FORMAT command instructs the system to load the FORMAT program into memory from subdirectory DOS on the disk in the default drive (drive C).
3. Press the Enter key after the FORMAT program displays the prompt messages to format the diskette in drive A.
4. Enter N to exit the FORMAT program.
5. With C> as the prompt, enter the following DOS commands:

   ```
   C>CD DOS
   C>FORMAT A:
   ```

   The CD command changes the current directory of the disk in the default drive (drive C) to subdirectory DOS. The FORMAT program is then loaded into memory and executed from the current directory of the default drive—in this case, subdirectory DOS on the disk in drive C.
6. Press the Enter key after the FORMAT program displays the prompt messages to format the diskette in drive A.
7. Enter N to exit the FORMAT program.

Note: The above steps illustrate two ways in which an external DOS command can be executed from a subdirectory of a disk.

BACKING UP AND RESTORING FILES ON A FIXED DISK

The **BACKUP** command allows you to copy (back up) one or more files from a fixed disk to a diskette. The **RESTORE** command allows you to copy (restore) one or more files from a diskette used with the BACKUP command to a fixed disk. For more information about these commands you should refer to Appendix B.

9 Customizing a System Using Batch Files

This chapter introduces information that allows you to automate some of the processes presented in previous chapters. The automation process utilizes batch files. The batch file concept, the AUTOEXEC.BAT file, the ECHO and REM commands, and the DOS utility program EDLIN are presented in this chapter. ECHO and REM are internal DOS commands (batch processing subcommands).

WHAT IS A BATCH FILE?

A **batch file** is a text file that contains DOS commands and has .BAT as the extension of the file name. When the name of a batch file is entered at command level, DOS executes the commands in the file. A **batch command** is the name of a batch file entered at command level. Note that you may break out of the execution of any batch command by entering Ctrl-Break or Ctrl-C (hold the Ctrl key down and press the Break key or the C key).

THE AUTOEXEC.BAT FILE

Each time you boot (start or restart) your system, the DOS command processor searches the root directory of the disk that is used in the boot process for a file named AUTOEXEC.BAT. The **AUTOEXEC.BAT file** is a special type of batch file that is automatically executed by DOS each time you boot your system.

An AUTOEXEC.BAT file allows you to execute a fixed set of DOS commands every time you boot your system.

AUTOEXEC.BAT for an Application Program Diskette

The AUTOEXEC.BAT file can be used on an application diskette to help automate the execution of an application such as word processing. Assume that DOS is installed on your word processing system diskette so that it is a bootable diskette. When you boot your system with this diskette, you normally respond to date and time prompts before DOS displays the system prompt. At this point you enter the name of the word processing program you want to execute—say, WP. The following steps show you how to create an AUTOEXEC.BAT file on this diskette that will boot your system into the word processing program.

1. Insert the working copy of your word processing system diskette in drive A.
2. With A> as the prompt, use the COPY CON command (see Chapter 7) to copy the following lines of text to the file AUTOEXEC.BAT in the root directory of the diskette in drive A:

   ```
   DATE
   TIME
   WP
   ```

3. Use Ctrl-Alt-Del to reboot (restart) your system.

   Note that the commands in the AUTOEXEC.BAT file are executed automatically. After you are prompted for the date and time, DOS executes the WP command, which begins your word processing program.

AUTOEXEC.BAT for a Fixed Disk

The AUTOEXEC.BAT file can be used on a fixed disk to help automate certain commands, like the PATH and PROMPT commands, each time you boot the system. The PATH command will be used to set the search path to the DOS subdirectory created in Chapter 8 (see Fig. 8.2). The PROMPT command will be used to change the standard DOS prompt to a prompt that includes the current directory specification.

1. With C> as the prompt, use the COPY CON command (see Chapter 7) to copy the following lines of text to the file AUTOEXEC.BAT in the root directory of the fixed disk:

   ```
   DATE
   TIME
   PATH C:\DOS
   PROMPT $P$G
   ```

2. Use Ctrl-Alt-Del to reboot (restart) your system.

   Note that the commands in the AUTOEXEC.BAT file are executed automatically. After you are prompted for the date and time, DOS executes the PATH command to set a search path and the PROMPT command to change the DOS prompt.

MODIFYING A BATCH FILE WITH EDLIN

EDLIN (EDit LINe or LINe EDitor) is a DOS utility program that allows you to create, edit (modify), and display text files. In this section, EDLIN will be used to modify the AUTOEXEC.BAT file that was created in the previous section and stored in the root directory of your fixed disk in drive C. Assume that your system was booted from the fixed disk, that the search path is set to C:\DOS, and that the DOS prompt displays the current directory specification. Also assume that the EDLIN program is in subdirectory DOS. (See Fig. 8.2).

1. With C:\> as the prompt, enter the following command:

   ```
   C:\>EDLIN AUTOEXEC.BAT
   ```

   After the EDLIN utility program is loaded into memory from subdirectory DOS on the fixed disk, EDLIN displays the following message followed by an asterisk (*), the EDLIN prompt:

   ```
   End of input file
   *
   ```

2. With * as the prompt, enter L.

   L instructs the EDLIN program to list (display) the contents of the AUTOEXEC.BAT file on the screen. EDLIN displays the following information:

   ```
   1:*DATE
   2: TIME
   3: PATH C:\DOS
   4: PROMPT $P$G
   ```

   Note that each line of information is prefaced by a line number followed by a colon (:). The asterisk (*) immediately after 1: indicates that line 1 is the current line number.

   Assume that you want to add a remark at the beginning of the file, that you do not want some of the commands displayed during execution, and that you want to have the current version of DOS displayed after the date and time prompts.

3. With * as the prompt, enter 1I.

   1I instructs the EDLIN program to insert lines beginning with line 1. The EDLIN program displays the following prompt:

   ```
   1:*
   ```

4. Enter the following remark after this prompt:

   ```
   REM ** AUTOEXEC.BAT is being executed. **
   ```

   The EDLIN program displays the following prompt:

   ```
   2:*
   ```

5. Enter the following batch command after the prompt:

```
ECHO OFF
```

The EDLIN program responds with:

```
3:*
```

This response indicates that the EDLIN program is still in insert mode.
6. Enter Ctrl-Break or Ctrl-C to break out of EDLIN's insert mode.
7. With * as the prompt, enter L to list the entire file.
8. With * as the prompt, enter 5I to insert a line at line 5.
9. After the EDLIN program prompts you with 5:*, enter VER.
10. After the EDLIN program prompts you with 6:*, enter Ctrl-Break or Ctrl-C to break out of EDLIN's insert mode.
11. With * as the prompt, enter L to list the entire file.

    The EDLIN program lists the following lines:

```
1: REM ** AUTOEXEC.BAT is being executed **
2: ECHO OFF
3: DATE
4: TIME
5: VER
6:*PATH C:\DOS
7: PROMPT $P$G
```

12. With * as the prompt, enter E to exit the EDLIN program.

    E allows you to end (exit, terminate) the execution of the EDLIN program. It also instructs EDLIN to rename the original file to AUTOEXEC.BAK (BAcKup) and to save the modified file as AUTOEXEC.BAT.
13. Use Ctrl-Alt-Del to reboot (restart) your system.

    Note the results of the new AUTOEXEC.BAT file.
14. With C:\> as the prompt, enter the following DOS command:

```
C:\>EDLIN AUTOEXEC.BAT
```

15. With * as the prompt, enter L to list the entire file.
16. With * as the prompt, enter 2D to delete line 2.
17. With * as the prompt, enter L to list the entire file.
18. With * as the prompt, enter E to exit the EDLIN program.
19. Use Ctrl-Alt-Del to reboot your system.

    Note that when the ECHO OFF command is not in the AUTOEXEC.BAT file, the DATE, TIME, VER, PATH, and PROMPT commands are displayed when they are executed from the batch file.

Note about the ECHO Command: The **ECHO** command controls the screen display of DOS commands executed from a batch file. ECHO is an internal batch processing subcommand.

Note about the EDLIN Utility Program: For more information about EDLIN, refer to the EDLIN command in Appendix B.

HANDY BATCH FILES WHEN USING A FIXED DISK

Assume that your fixed disk in drive C contains the directory structure given in Fig. 8.2. With this structure, if you want to do word processing, you change the current directory to subdirectory WP and run the word processing program. When you exit the word processing program, the current directory is subdirectory WP. To do a spreadsheet application, you need to change the current directory to subdirectory SS and run the spreadsheet program. When you exit the spreadsheet program, the current directory is subdirectory SS. This process must be repeated for each application program that you run from the fixed disk. You can make the process of running application programs from your fixed disk much more convenient by building a short batch file to execute for each application program.

A Batch File to Run MultiMate

Assume that you use the MultiMate word processor and that the MultiMate programs are in subdirectory WP of the fixed disk in drive C. Also assume that the current directory of the fixed disk is the root directory.

1. With C> as the prompt, use the COPY CON command (see Chapter 7) to copy the following lines of text to the file MMB.BAT (MultiMate Batch file) in the root directory of the fixed disk:

   ```
   CD WP
   WP
   CD \
   ```

2. With C> as the prompt, enter MMB.

   When the batch file MMB.BAT is executed, the current directory is changed to WP before the MultiMate program is executed. When you exit the MultiMate program, the current directory is changed back to the root directory of the fixed disk.

A Batch File to Run WordPerfect

Assume that you use the WordPerfect word processor, that the WordPerfect programs are in subdirectory WP of the fixed disk in drive C, and that the WordPerfect data diskette is in drive A. Also assume that the current directory of the fixed disk is the root directory.

1. With C> as the prompt, use the COPY CON command (see Chapter 7) to copy the following lines of text to the file WPB.BAT (WordPerfect Batch file) in the root directory of the fixed disk:

```
CD WP
A:
C:WP
C:
CD \
CLS
```

2. With C> as the prompt, enter WPB.

   When the batch file WPB.BAT is executed, the current directory of drive C is changed to WP, and the default drive is changed to drive A—in this case, the WordPerfect data diskette drive. The WordPerfect program is then loaded into memory from drive C and executed. When you exit the WordPerfect program, the default drive is changed back to drive C and the current directory is changed back to the root directory of the fixed disk. The last command in the batch file clears your screen.

A Batch File to Run Lotus 1-2-3

Assume that you use the Lotus 1-2-3 spreadsheet application and that the Lotus 1-2-3 programs are in subdirectory SS of the fixed disk in drive C. Also assume that the current directory of the fixed disk is the root directory.

1. With C> as the prompt, use the COPY CON command (see Chapter 7) to copy the following lines of text to the file LOTB.BAT (LOTus Batch File) in the root directory of the fixed disk:

```
CD SS
LOTUS
CD \
```

2. With C> as the prompt, enter LOTB.

   When the batch file LOTB.BAT is executed, the current directory is changed to SS before the Lotus program is executed. When you exit the Lotus program, the current directory is changed to the root directory of the fixed disk.

Appendix A: DOS Command Notation and Special Keys

TABLE A.1 NOTATION USED IN DESCRIBING DOS COMMANDS

Notation	Description
`UPPERCASE LETTERS`	Words in uppercase letters in DOS commands are called keywords. DOS command names are shown in uppercase letters and are keywords. In the DOS command format descriptions, uppercase letters and uppercase words may be entered on the command line in any combination of uppercase and lowercase letters.
`lowercase italic letters`	Command items shown in lowercase italic letters indicate that you are to substitute your information for these items.

UPPERCASE ITALIC LETTERS

Used in examples to indicate DOS prompts that are displayed on the screen.

[ ]

Items shown within square brackets indicate optional parameters for a command. If you decide to include the optional parameters, do not include the square brackets in the command.

{ }

Items shown within braces indicate that one and only one of the items inside the braces can appear in the command. The items are separated by a vertical bar. Do not include the braces in the command.

|

The vertical bar is used to separate items contained within braces or square brackets. One and only one of the items separated by the vertical bar can be used in the command.

¦

The split vertical bar indicates piping of output and input. This character is used between two DOS commands and instructs DOS to pipe (send) the output from the first (left) command to the second command as input.

<

The "less than" symbol is the standard input redirection operator. Input data for the command specified to the left of the symbol is received from the file or device specified to the right of the symbol. The format is `command < filespec`.

>

The "greater than" symbol is the standard output redirection operator. The output information generated by the command specified to the left of the symbol is sent to the file or device specified to the right of the symbol. The format is `command > filespec`.

...

Ellipsis points (repeat indicators) show that the items following the first unmatched left bracket can be repeated any number of times. Do not include the ellipsis points in the command.

Other Symbols

Any other symbols or number on the command line must be typed exactly as shown.

TABLE A.2 TERMS USED IN DESCRIBING DOS COMMANDS

Term	**Description**
command	A DOS command.
command line	A command line consists of [*pathspec*] *command* [*parameters*] where *pathspec* specifies the drive and the pathname in which *command* is located, *command* is a DOS command, and *parameters* denote any additional information appearing on the command line.
parameter	A parameter is any item appearing on a command line after the DOS command name. Parameters reside in fields that are separated by command line delimiters such as spaces, commas, and slashes.
d: *d1: d2: d3:*	d: is a drive designator. When a command contains multiple drive specifications within its parameter list, *d1:*, *d2:*, and *d3:* may be used as drive designators to aid in the description of the command.
filename	*filename* denotes the first part of the name of a file and consists of at least one and up to eight of the following characters: A-Z a-z 0-9 $ & # @ ! % - _ ' ( ) { } DOS does not distinguish between uppercase and lowercase characters in a filename.
.*ext*	.*ext* denotes a filename extension or the second part of the name of a file and consists of a period followed by one to three valid *filename* characters. Filename extensions are optional.
file name	A file name consists of *filename*[.*ext*].
wildcard (global) file name characters	The characters * and ? are called wildcard (global) file name characters. * can be used to represent zero or more characters at the end of a filename or filename extension, and ? can be used to represent a single character in a filename or filename extension. The wildcard characters can be used in file names in many DOS commands.

filespec *filespec1* *filespec2* *filespec3*	*filespec* denotes the file specification [*d:*] [*pathname*] *filename* [.*ext*], which is equivalent to [*pathspec*] *filename* [.*ext*]. In a few cases, to simplify notation, *filespec* may be used to denote [*d:*] [*pathname*] [*filename*] [.*ext*]. When a command contains multiple file specifications within its parameter list, *filespec1*, *filespec2*, and *filespec3* may be used as file specifications to aid in the description of the command.
subdirname	*subdirname* denotes a subdirectory name on a disk. *subdirname* has the same format and valid character set as a file name.
directory path	A directory path or path is the route you must follow to trace your way from the disk's main or root directory to a particular place in the directory structure.
pathname	*pathname* denotes the directory search path [\] [*subdirname*] [*subdirname*] ...]. It specifies a series of subdirectory names separated by backslashes (\). A *pathname* beginning with a backslash states that the directory search path begins with the root directory. A *pathname* beginning with a double period (..) states that the directory search path begins with the parent directory of the current directory.
pathspec	*pathspec* denotes the path specification [*d:*]*pathname*.

TABLE A.3 SPECIAL DOS CONTROL KEYS

Control Key	Description of Action
`Ctrl-Alt-Del`	Instructs DOS to start a warm system boot (restart or reset DOS).
`Ctrl-Break` `Ctrl-C`	Instructs DOS to cancel whatever the system or a program is doing and return you to command level.
`Ctrl-NumLock`	Instructs DOS to suspend (halt) whatever the system is doing until you press another key.
`Ctrl-PrtSc` `Ctrl-P`	Acts as a printer echo switch. Pressing Ctrl-PrtSc (Ctrl-P) the first time instructs DOS to turn the echo mode on. That is, DOS starts printing every line at the same time as it is being displayed on the screen. Pressing Ctrl-PrtSc (Ctrl-P) a second time instructs DOS to turn the printer echo mode off.
`Ctrl-S`	Instructs DOS to suspend output to the display unit (screen).
`Ctrl-Z` `F6`	Ctrl-Z generates an end-of-file marker. This can also be accomplished by pressing the F6 function key.
`Shift-PrtSc`	Instructs DOS to copy the information that is currently displayed on the screen to the printer.

Note: When you key in the characters for a DOS command, they are stored in a temporary storage area called the **command line buffer** or **keyboard buffer**. DOS always displays the contents of the command line (keyboard) buffer. The system processes the command line buffer after you press the Enter key. Pressing the Enter key initiates three tasks.

1. The contents of the command line buffer are sent to COMMAND.COM for interpretation and execution.
2. The command line buffer is copied into another temporary storage area called the **template**.
3. The command line buffer is cleared.

The last DOS command you entered is usually saved in the template, but not all commands are saved in the template.

TABLE A.4 DOS EDITING AND FUNCTION KEYS

Editing Key	Editing Key Description
`F1` `Right arrow`	Copies the next character from the template to the command line buffer.
`F2 c`	Copies all characters up to (not including) the specified character *c* from the template to the command line buffer.
`F3`	Copies all remaining characters in the template to the command line buffer.
`F4 c`	Skips over (does not copy) the characters in the template up to (not including) the specified character *c*.
`F5`	Copies the command line buffer to the template and clears the command line buffer.

`Left arrow`
`Back space`
`Back arrow`
	Erases (deletes) the previous character from the command line buffer without changing the template.

`Esc`	Clears the command line buffer without changing the template.
`Ins`	Puts DOS in insert mode. This allows you to enter characters from the keyboard without changing the current reference position in the template.
`Del`	Skips over (does not copy) a character in the template.
`NumLock`	Activates the numeric key pad mode or activates the arrow key/special function key mode. It is used to toggle between these two modes.

Appendix B: DOS Version 3.30 Commands

INTERNAL VERSUS EXTERNAL DOS COMMANDS

DOS commands are separated into two fundamental categories, internal DOS commands and external DOS commands. DOS commands that are resident in main memory after you boot your system are referred to as **internal DOS commands**. All other DOS commands are categorized as **external DOS commands**.

This means that any internal DOS command is always available for use at command level. When an external DOS command is used, the system routine associated with that command does not reside in main memory and must be available to the system on some external media such as a diskette or a fixed disk. Consequently, when you use an external DOS command, you must make sure that the appropriate path specification is given so that this command can be referenced, loaded into memory, and executed by the system. This may be accomplished by having the DOS diskette in the default disk drive.

Table B.1 gives a complete list of the DOS Version 3.30 commands described in this appendix. It also indicates the following:

1. DOS 3.xx commands that are the same as DOS 2.xx commands.
2. DOS 3.xx commands that contain modifications of the corresponding DOS 2.xx commands.

3. DOS 3.xx commands that are not available in DOS 2.xx.
4. DOS 3.30 commands that contain modifications of the corresponding commands in previous versions of DOS.
5. DOS 3.30 commands that are not available in previous versions of DOS.

Note that the commands are separated into three categories: internal DOS commands, internal DOS batch processing subcommands, and external DOS commands.

TABLE B.1 DOS COMMANDS BY NAME

Notation Used in the Table: Commands marked V3 are not available in versions of DOS prior to Version 3. Commands marked V3m are available in versions of DOS prior to Version 3, but have been modified in DOS Version 3. Commands marked V3.2 (V3.3) are new commands available in DOS Version 3.20 (3.30) that are not available in previous versions of DOS. Finally, commands marked with an asterisk (*) have been modified in DOS Version 3.30. Commands that are not marked have remained fundamentally unchanged through all versions of DOS. The internal batch commands have been listed separately, owing to differences in their use.

Internal DOS Commands

	Command		Command
	BREAK		MKDIR (MD)
V3.3	CHCP		PATH
	CHDIR (CD)		PROMPT
	CLS		RENAME (REN)
	COPY		RMDIR (RD)
	CTTY		SET
V3m *	DATE	*	TIME
	DEL (ERASE)		TYPE
	DIR		VER
	ERASE (DEL)		VERIFY
	EXIT		VOL

Internal DOS Commands (Batch Processing Subcommands)

	Command		Command
V3.3	CALL		IF
*	ECHO		PAUSE
	FOR %%		REM
	GOTO		SHIFT

External DOS Commands

```
V3.3    APPEND (also internal)         V3      JOIN
        ASSIGN                         V3   * KEYB
V3   *  ATTRIB                         V3      LABEL
V3m  *  BACKUP                         V3m  * MODE
V3m  *  Batch (.BAT)                           MORE
        CHKDSK                         V3.3    NLSFUNC
V3      COMMAND                        V3m     PRINT
        COMP                                   RECOVER
V3m     DISKCOMP                       V3.2    REPLACE
V3m     DISKCOPY                       V3m  * RESTORE
        EDLIN (DOS Utility)            V3      SELECT
        EXE2BIN (Not in DOS 3.30)      V3      SHARE
V3.3    FASTOPEN                               SORT
V3m  *  FDISK                          V3      SUBST
        FIND                                   SYS
V3m  *  FORMAT                                 TREE
V3   *  GRAFTABL                       V3.2    XCOPY
V3m  *  GRAPHICS
```

NOTATION USED FOR COMMAND FORMATS

The way that a command is presented in Appendix B is not the way that you would enter the command at the keyboard. Lowercase italic letters and words that appear in the format of a command description represent information that must be supplied by you when you use that command. For example, consider the following command format for the RENAME command:

RENAME *filespec filename*[*.ext*]

When you use the RENAME command, you must specify the file to be renamed (denoted by *filespec*) and the new file name (denoted by *filename*[*.ext*]), which has an optional filename extension. The following example illustrates an explicit use of the RENAME command to rename a file:

```
RENAME A:FORMAT.COM FRMT.COM
```

Italic characters are also used in the example section of a command description to denote DOS prompts. You should refer to Appendix A for a complete listing of the notation used in Appendix B.

APPEND (SET PATHS FOR NONEXECUTABLE FILES)

Format `APPEND` *pathspec*`[;`*pathspec* `...]` or
`APPEND [/X][/E]` or
`APPEND [;]`

Type External (first time APPEND is loaded and executed)
Internal (after APPEND has been executed the first time)

Summary APPEND instructs DOS where to search for data files that it does not find in the current directory.

Remarks
- APPEND is a new feature of DOS 3.30.
- /X instructs APPEND to process SEARCH FIRST, FIND FIRST, and EXEC functions.
- /E instructs APPEND to keep the APPEND *pathspecs* in the DOS environment.
- /X and /E can be specified only on the first execution of the APPEND command.
- APPEND specifies one or more *pathspecs* that DOS uses to search for nonexecutable files not found in the current directory. The PATH command instructs DOS where to search for files having an extension of .COM, .EXE, or .BAT that are not found in the current directory. APPEND instructs DOS where to search for files not having one of these extensions.
- If the only parameter following the APPEND is a semicolon, then APPEND resets the pathspec list to null.

ASSIGN (CHANGE/RESET DISK DRIVE ASSIGNMENTS)

Format `ASSIGN [`*d1*`[=]`*d2*`[...]]`

Type External

Summary ASSIGN instructs DOS to convert disk I/O (Input/Output) requests for drive *d1* into disk I/O requests for drive *d2*.

Remarks
- Both drives *d1* and *d2* must exist on your system.
- When the ASSIGN command is used with no parameters, all disk drive assignments are reset to the normal drive assignments.

Example The following command converts every I/O reference of drive A and drive B to a reference of drive C:

```
A>ASSIGN A=C B=C
```

ATTRIB (SET/RESET/DISPLAY READ-ONLY ATTRIBUTE AND ARCHIVE BIT)

Format `ATTRIB [+R | -R][+A | -A] filespec[/S]`

Type External

Cited Chapter 5

Summary ATTRIB allows you to set the read-only file attribute on or off, to set the archive bit on or off, and to display the current settings of these attributes. The ATTRIB command operates upon a file or set of files specified by *filespec*.

Remarks

- +R instructs ATTRIB to make *filespec* read-only (cannot be modified or deleted).
- -R instructs ATTRIB to remove the read-only attribute of *filespec* (can be modified or deleted).
- +A instructs ATTRIB to set the archive bit on for *filespec*.
- -A instructs ATTRIB to set the archive bit off for *filespec*.
- /S instructs ATTRIB to process all files in the specified directory and its subdirectories. (New feature of DOS 3.30)
- The commands BACKUP /M and XCOPY /M copy a file only if its archive bit is set on.
- When you create a new file, its read-only attribute is set off and the archive attribute bit is set on.
- When *filespec* is the only specified parameter, ATTRIB displays the read-only status (R) and the archive bit status (A) for each file included in *filespec*.

Example The following command sets the read-only attribute on and the archive attribute bit off for the file TEST.DOC:

```
A>ATTRIB +R -A TEST.DOC
```

BACKUP (BACK UP FILES)

Format `BACKUP` *`d1`*`:[`*`filespec`*`]` *`d2`*`:[/S][/M][/A]`
`[/D:`*`mm-dd-yy`*`][/T:`*`hh:mm:ss`*`]`
`[/F][/L[`*`pathspec`*`]]`

Type External

Cited Chapter 8

Summary BACKUP allows you to back up one or more files from a disk in drive *d1* (source disk) to a disk in a different drive *d2* (target disk).

Remarks

- /S requests the backup of subdirectory files in addition to the files in the specified or current directory.
- /M requests the backup of files that have been modified since the last backup.
- /A requests that the file(s) being backed up be added to the files already present on the target disk. If this option is not used, the directory of the target disk is erased before any files are backed up.
- /D:*mm-dd-yy* requests the backup of files that have creation or modification dates on or after the specified date, *mm-dd-yy*.
- /T requests the backup of files that have been modified on or after the specified time on the specified date. (New feature of DOS 3.30)
- /F instructs DOS to format the target diskette if it is not already formatted. (New feature of DOS 3.30)
- /L requests BACKUP to create a log file. (New feature of DOS 3.30)
- The BACKUP command should not be used while APPEND is in effect. (New feature of DOS 3.30)

Batch [.BAT] (CALL BATCH FILE FOR EXECUTION)

Format `[`*`pathspec`*`]`*`filename`*`[.BAT][`*`parameters`*`]`

Type External

Cited Chapter 9

Summary A Batch command consists of a *filename* with extension .BAT which references a special file containing DOS commands. This special file is called a batch file. When the name of a batch file is used as a command, the DOS commands that are included in the file are executed in sequence.

Remarks • There are eight subcommands that can be used in a batch file to control batch processing. They are CALL, ECHO, FOR, GOTO, IF, PAUSE, REM, and SHIFT.

• Each time you boot the system, DOS searches the root directory of the boot disk for a special file named AUTOEXEC.BAT. If a file named AUTOEXEC.BAT is in the root directory of the boot disk, it is automatically executed each time the system is booted.

BREAK (SET/DISPLAY CONTROL BREAK CHECKING STATUS)

Format `BREAK [ON | OFF]`

Type Internal

Summary BREAK ON instructs DOS to check for a control break (Ctrl-C) whenever a program calls on DOS to perform any function. BREAK OFF instructs DOS not to check for a control break. BREAK followed by no parameters instructs DOS to display the current state (ON or OFF) of the BREAK command.

Remarks • The system normally starts up with BREAK set to OFF, unless it is set ON in a CONFIG.SYS or AUTOEXEC.BAT file.

CALL (CALL A BATCH FILE)

Format `CALL` *`filespec`*

Type Internal, batch processing subcommand

Summary CALL allows the batch file, *filespec*, to be called from within another batch file without ending the first batch file.

Remarks • CALL is a new feature of DOS 3.30.

CHCP (CHANGE THE CODE PAGE)

Format `CHCP [`*`code-page`*`]`

Type Internal

Summary CHCP allows you to change the code page that DOS will use to the specified *code-page* number or to display the active code page number.

Remarks • CHCP is a new feature of DOS 3.30.

• CHCP allows you to change the characters displayed on a display screen or printed on a device.

• If *code-page* is not specified, the active code page number is displayed.

CHDIR [CD] (CHANGE/DISPLAY CURRENT DIRECTORY)

Format `CHDIR [pathspec]` or
`CD [pathspec]`

Type Internal

Cited Chapters 8, 9

Summary CHDIR (CD) instructs DOS to change the current directory to the specified directory given by *pathspec* or to display the pathspec of the current directory.

Remarks • Each disk drive has a current directory associated with it. DOS keeps track of the current directory for each drive in the system.

• To change the current directory of a drive other than the current drive, you enter the CHDIR (CD) command with the drive designator and pathname of the desired new current directory for the specified drive.

• A leading backslash (\) in a pathname tells DOS to begin the path at the root directory.

• The pathname specification cannot be longer than 63 characters starting from the root directory.

CHKDSK (CHECK DISK)

Format `CHKDSK [d:][pathname][filename[.ext]][/F][/V]`

Type External

Cited Chapters 4, 8

Summary CHKDSK analyzes the directories, files, and File Allocation Table (FAT) on the designated or default drive and displays a disk and memory status report. If you specify *filename* in the command, CHKDSK displays the number of noncontiguous areas occupied by the file or files.

Remarks • /F specifies the Fix parameter and instructs CHKDSK to try to correct any errors that it finds in the directory or file allocation table.

• /V specifies the View parameter and instructs CHKDSK to display the pathspecs of directories and the filespecs of files that have been checked. This listing includes any hidden files that may be on the disk and the disk's volume label if it exists.

• The CHKDSK status report for a bootable disk with a volume label shows at least three hidden files: the volume label and the DOS system files IBMBIO.COM and IBMDOS.COM. These hidden files do not appear in normal directory searches. Some application programs also create hidden files.

• You can use *.* in place of *filename.ext* in the CHKDSK command to determine the extent of file fragmentation on a disk.

• You should run CHKDSK occassionally for each fixed disk drive and frequently used diskettes. This helps to ensure the integrity of the file structure and checks for file fragmentation.

CLS (CLEAR SCREEN)

Format `CLS`

Type Internal

Cited Chapter 2

Summary CLS clears all displayed information from the screen except the system prompt, which appears in the upper left-hand corner of the screen.

COMMAND (START SECONDARY COMMAND PROCESSOR)

Format

```
COMMAND [d:][pathname][/P][/C string]
        [/E: size]
```

Type External

Summary COMMAND starts a secondary command processor. That is, the COMMAND command loads a copy of a new command processor, COMMAND.COM, into memory.

Remarks
- /P instructs DOS to make the copy of the new command processor permanent in memory. This means that the secondary command processor does not return to the primary command processor.
- *string* denotes a DOS command that you want to pass to the command processor.
- /C *string* allows you to pass a DOS command (*string*) to the secondary command processor, execute *string*, and automatically return your system to the primary command processor.
- /E: *size* allows you to set the environment size to *size* where *size* is a decimal integer between 160 and 32,768.
- When a secondary command processor is loaded with no parameters specified, you can return control to the previous level command processor by using the EXIT command.

COMP (COMPARE TWO SETS OF FILES)

Format `COMP [filespec1] [filespec2]`

Type External

Cited Chapter 6

Summary COMP allows you to compare the contents of two files or two sets of files and display their differences. The file(s) denoted by *filespec1* (primary file(s)) are compared against the file(s) denoted by *filespec2* (secondary file(s)).

Remarks
- The paths and the names of the files being compared are displayed as they are compared.
- Wildcard characters can be used in the file specifications. They allow you to specify groups of files to be compared instead of two files at a time.
- The comparison operation is not performed if the sizes of the two files being compared do not match.
- You can compare all the files in one directory with all the corresponding files in another directory.
- If *filespec1* and *filespec2* are not specified or if *filespec2* is not specified, COMP prompts you for this information.
- COMP will display error messages whenever information does not match.

COPY (COPY NAMED FILES)

Format `COPY [/A][/B]`*filespec*`[/A][/B] [`*filespec2*`]`
`[/A][/B][/V]` or
`COPY [/A][/B]`*filespec*`[/A][/B] [+`*filespec1*
`[/A][/B]...] [`*filespec2*`][/A][/B][/V]` or
`COPY CON {`*filespec* `| PRN}`

Type Internal

Cited Chapters 3, 5–9

Summary COPY instructs DOS to copy one or more specified files to the default or specified disk. COPY copies files only from the current or specified directory. *filespec* (and *filespec1*) specifies the source file(s) or source group of files to be copied. *filespec2* specifies the target file or target path. The COPY CON command instructs DOS to copy input from the keyboard console (CON) to *filespec* or the printer (PRN).

Remarks

- The parameters /A and /B apply to the *filespec* immediately preceding it and to all remaining filespecs in the command until another /A or /B is encountered.
- /A (with a source *filespec*) indicates that the file is to be treated as a text or ASCII file. A Ctrl-Z (1A hexadecimal) is interpreted as the end-of-file marker. The file is copied up to, but not including, the first end-of-file marker. Also, the file is not copied beyond the end-of-file marker.
- /A (with a target *filespec2*) instructs COPY to place a Ctrl-Z character (end-of-file marker) as the last character in the target file.
- /B (with a source *filespec*) indicates that the file is to be treated as a binary file. The entire file as specified in directory file size (including Ctrl-Z characters) is copied up to the physical end-of-file.
- /B (with a target *filespec2*) instructs COPY to not place an end-of-file marker (Ctrl-Z) at the end of the target file.
- /V instructs COPY to verify that the source and target files are identical, after copying.
- \+ indicates that COPY is to perform concatenation of files.
- When a read-only file is copied with the COPY command, the read-only status is not transferred to the target file.
- The COPY command can be used to combine two or more files into one file by adding the additional files to the end of the first file. Combining files is normally done in the text (or ASCII) mode.
- When the COPY CON command is used, an end-of-file marker (Ctrl-Z) must be entered to complete the copying process.

CTTY (CHANGE STANDARD INPUT/OUTPUT CONSOLE)

Format `CTTY` *`device`*

Type Internal

Summary CTTY allows you to change the standard I/O (Input/Output) console to an auxiliary console or to restore the keyboard and the display screen as the standard input and output devices, respectively.

Remarks
- The parameter *device* denotes any character-oriented device and is used to specify the primary console. When the specified *device* is AUX, COM1, COM2, COM3, or COM4, that device becomes the primary console. When the specified *device* is CON, the standard input and output devices (the keyboard and the display screen) are reset to the primary console.

Example If you want DOS to use the AUX device for keyboard and display operations, use the command

```
A>CTTY AUX
```

- If you want DOS to switch back to the standard keyboard and display screen as the primary console, use the command

```
A>CTTY CON
```

DATE (DISPLAY/SET CURRENT DATE)

Format `DATE [`*`mm-dd-yy | dd-mm-yy | yy-mm-dd`*`]`

Type Internal

Cited Chapters 2, 9

Summary DATE instructs DOS to display and set the system date where *mm* specifies the month (1 through 12), *dd* specifies the day (1 through 31), and *yy* specifies the year (80 through 99 or 1980 through 1999).

Remarks
- If you enter DATE with no parameters, the current system date and a prompt message are displayed on the screen. At this point you may either accept the current date or enter a new date.
- The parts of the date may be separated with a dash (-), a slash (/), or a period (.).
- When a file is created or modified, the current system date and time are recorded in the directory with the file name.
- If you have a real-time clock/calendar on your system, the DATE command in DOS 3.30 changes both the system date and the

clock/calendar date. The DATE command in DOS versions previous to DOS 3.30 will not change the clock/calendar date.

DEL (DELETE/ERASE NAMED FILES)

Format DEL *filespec*

Type Internal

Cited Chapters 5, 8

Summary DEL instructs DOS to delete (erase) *filespec* from the directory of the disk.

Remarks
- The DEL and ERASE commands perform the same operations.
- The DEL command does not destroy or remove the information in *filespec*; it only marks the file name(s) in the disk's directory as a deleted (erased) file(s).
- DEL will not delete files that are marked as read-only files.
- Wildcard characters may be used in *filespec*. Before using DEL with wildcard characters in *filespec*, enter the command DIR *filespec* to obtain a list of the files that will be deleted.
- DEL should be used with extreme care after using ASSIGN, JOIN, or SUBST.
- DEL will not delete hidden files such as IBMBIO.COM and IBMDOS.COM.
- If the parameter of the DEL command is a path specification, DEL deletes all files in the specified directory.

DIR (DISPLAY DIRECTORY INFORMATION)

Format `DIR [filespec][/P][/W]`

Type Internal

Cited Chapters 4, 5, 7, 8

Summary DIR instructs DOS to display all directory entries (file and subdirectory names) in the current or specified directory, or to display only the directory entries specified by *filespec*. Directory entries for hidden files (such as IBMBIO.COM and IBMDOS.COM) are not displayed by the DIR command.

Remarks
- The general information produced by the DIR command includes the volume label (if it exists), the number of directory entries displayed,

and the amount of free space left on the disk (rounded up to the nearest 1024 bytes).

- The information produced for files includes filenames, extensions, file size in bytes, and the date and time that each file was created or last modified. The DIR command identifies subdirectories by displaying <DIR> after each subdirectory name.
- /P (Pause) instructs DIR to pause the listing of directory information when the display screen is full. Pressing any key continues the listing.
- /W (Wide display format) instructs DIR to display five filenames with extensions or subdirectory names on each line. The file size and date and subdirectory markers do not appear in this format.

DISKCOMP (COMPARE DISKETTES)

Format `DISKCOMP [d1: [d2:]][/1][/8]`

Type External

Cited Chapter 6

Summary DISKCOMP allows you to compare the contents of the diskette in drive *d1* (source drive) to the contents of the diskette in drive *d2* (target drive).

Remarks

- /1 instructs DISKCOMP that you want to compare only the first side of each diskette, regardless of the format of each diskette and the drive type.
- /8 instructs DISKCOMP that you want to compare only 8 sectors per track, regardless of the number of sectors per track on each diskette.
- The DISKCOMP command should be used to compare two entire diskettes on a track-by-track basis. The COMP command should be used to compare files to each other.
- If no side or track parameters are specified, DISKCOMP automatically determines the number of sides and sectors per track that can be read from the source diskette (diskette in drive *d1*). These characteristics are used in the comparison with the target diskette (diskette in drive *d2*).
- DISKCOMP does not recognize assigned drives (ASSIGN), joined drives (JOIN), substituted drives (SUBST), or networked drives.
- DISKCOMP can be used only with compatible diskette drives and diskettes.

DISKCOPY (COPY DISKETTES)

Format `DISKCOPY [d1: [d2:]][/1]`

Type External

Cited Chapters 2, 5, 6

Summary DISKCOPY allows you to copy the entire contents of the diskette in drive *d1* (source drive) to the diskette in drive *d2* (target drive). If necessary, DISKCOPY will format the target diskette while copying.

Remarks

- /1 instructs DISKCOPY to copy only the first side of the source diskette, regardless of the diskette or drive type.
- The DISKCOPY command should be used to copy an entire diskette. The COPY command should be used to copy individual files.
- If /1 is not specified, DISKCOPY automatically determines, from the source diskette, the number of sides and sectors per track to copy.
- The source and target drives cannot be VDISKS, joined drives (JOIN), substituted drives (SUBST), or networked drives.
- If DISKCOPY determines an error in reading the source diskette or writing to the target diskette, it displays the track and side where the error occured but continues copying. If such an error occurs, bad data may have been transferred, making the target diskette unusable.
- DISKCOMP can be used after DISKCOPY has finished copying to determine whether the two diskettes are identical.

ECHO (SET/DISPLAY ECHO STATUS IN BATCH PROCESSING)

Format `ECHO [ON | OFF | message]`

Type Internal, batch processing subcommand

Cited Chapter 9

Summary ECHO controls the screen display of DOS commands executed from a batch file. Messages generated from the execution of batched DOS commands are not affected by the ECHO command.

Remarks • If the ECHO command is used without any parameters, the current ECHO setting (ON or OFF) is displayed.

• If a command line in a batch file begins with the @ character, that line is not displayed when it is executed in a batch file. (New feature of DOS 3.30)

EDLIN (CALL LINE EDITOR UTILITY)

Format `EDLIN filespec[/B]`

Type External (Utility program)

Cited Chapter 9

Summary The EDLIN command is used to invoke the line editor utility program. This program allows you to create, edit, and display text files.

Remarks • EDLIN is normally considered to be a DOS utility program and not a DOS command. It is included here because of its importance in creating and editing files.

• /B instructs EDLIN to load *filespec* up to the physical end-of-file. You should use this parameter when you know that *filespec* contains embedded end-of-file markers (Ctrl-Z). If you do not use the /B parameter, EDLIN uses *filespec* up to the first end-of-file marker (Ctrl-Z).

• The EDLIN prompt is an asterisk (*).

• The current line denotes the location of the last change to a file and is denoted by an asterisk immediately following the line number.

• Several fundamental EDLIN commands are listed below where n, n1, n2, and n3 are used to specify line numbers. This is not a complete set of EDLIN commands.

`[n1],[n2],n3[,count]C`	• Copies lines *n1* through *n2* to lines beginning with *n3*. *count* specifies the number of times the range is to be duplicated. *count* defaults to one.
`[n1][,n2]D`	• Deletes lines *n1* through *n2*.
`n`	• Allows you to edit line *n*.
`E`	• Ends EDLIN and saves the edited file as *filespec*. The original file that was specified in EDLIN is given a .BAK filename extension.

`[n]I`	• Inserts lines of text immediately before line *n*. When you are creating a new file, you must enter an I to insert text lines into the file. You can terminate the insert command by entering Ctrl-C (Ctrl-Break).
`[n1][,n2]L`	• List lines *n1* through *n2* on the display screen. If *n2* is omitted, lines *n1* to the end of the file are listed. When L is used with no line numbers, the entire file is listed.
`[n1],[n2],n3M`	• Moves lines *n1* through *n2* in front of line *n3*.
`Q`	• Quit (terminate) the EDLIN session without saving any changes.

ERASE (ERASE/DELETE NAMED FILES)

Format `ERASE filespec`

Type Internal

Cited Chapters 5, 8

Summary ERASE instructs DOS to erase (delete) *filespec* from the directory of the disk.

Remarks

- The ERASE and DEL commands perform the same operations.
- The ERASE command does not destroy or remove the information in *filespec*; it only marks the file name(s) in the disk's directory as an erased (deleted) file(s).
- ERASE will not erase files that are marked as read-only files.
- Wildcard characters may be used in *filespec*. Before using ERASE with wildcard characters in *filespec*, enter the command DIR *filespec* to obtain a list of the files that will be erased.
- ERASE should be used with extreme care after using ASSIGN, JOIN, or SUBST.
- ERASE will not erase hidden files such as IBMBIO.COM and IBMDOS.COM.
- If the parameter of the ERASE command is a path specification, ERASE erases all files in the specified directory.

EXE2BIN (CONVERT .EXE FILES TO BINARY)

Format `EXE2BIN` *filespec1* [*filespec2*]

Type External

Summary EXE2BIN allows you to convert *filespec1* (input file) from a relocatable EXE file to a memory-image COM file and places it in *filespec2* (output file).

Remarks
- Not all EXE files can be converted to a COM format. *filespec1* must be in valid EXE format as produced by the LINK program utility.
- The EXE2BIN command and the LINK program utility are not available in DOS 3.30.

EXIT (EXIT COMMAND PROCESSOR)

Format `EXIT`

Type Internal

Summary EXIT allows you to leave a nonpermanent COMMAND.COM command processor and return to the previous level command processor.

FASTOPEN (FAST ACCESS TO RECENTLY OPENED FILES)

Format `FASTOPEN` *d*: [=*num-dir*]

Type External

Summary FASTOPEN provides fast access of files on drive *d* by storing in memory the location of directories and recently opened files on drive *d*.

Remarks
- FASTOPEN is a new feature of DOS 3.30.
- *d*: may specify any fixed disk drive except assigned drives (ASSIGN), joined drives (JOIN), substituted drives (SUBST), and networked drives.
- *num-dir* specifies the number (between 10 and 999) of directories or file entries to save in memory for drive *d*. If *num-dir* is not specified, 34 is assumed.

FDISK (FIXED DISK PREPARATION)

Format `FDISK`

Type External

Cited Chapter 3

Summary The FDISK command is used to prepare a fixed disk. FDISK allows you to create a partition, delete a partition, change an active partition, or display partition information on a fixed disk.

Remarks
- A menu screen is displayed after the FDISK command is entered.
- A fixed disk can be divided into one, two, three, or four sections called partitions.
- When you make a partition active, the operating system residing within that partition is the operating system that is booted when the system is restarted from that drive.
- FDISK allows you to create multiple logical disk drives on a single large fixed disk system. Each logical drive can be any size up to 32MB. (New feature of DOS 3.30)

FIND (FIND TEXT STRING)

Format
```
FIND [/C][/N][/V] "string" filespec1
     [filespec2...]
```
or
```
command ¦ FIND [/C][/N][/V] "string"
```

Type External

Summary FIND allows you to locate and display all lines in the specified file(s) (*filespec1* [*filespec2*...]) that contain the specified *string*. Output from a DOS command may also be piped (¦) to the FIND command.

Remarks
- *string* specifies a sequence of characters that you want to find. *string* must be enclosed in double quotation marks ("). Two double quotation marks in succession are interpreted as one double quotation mark within *string*.
- /C instructs FIND to display the number of times that *string* appears in each specified file without displaying each line that contains *string*.
- /N instructs FIND to display the relative line number in front of each line that it displays.
- /V instructs FIND to display all lines in each specified file that do not contain *string*.

- If /C is specified with either /N or /V, then no lines of text are displayed. Only a count is displayed.
- You cannot use piping operators when the default disk is write-protected.
- You cannot use wildcard characters with the FIND command.

Example The following command will display all lines from FILE1.DOC and FILE2.DOC that contain the string "Programmer":

```
A>FIND "Programmer" FILE1.DOC FILE2.DOC
```

- The following command will display all file specifications in the directory of drive B that contain the string "EXE":

```
A>DIR B: ¦ FIND "EXE"
```

FOR %% (ITERATION CONSTRUCT IN BATCH PROCESSING)

Format `FOR %%v IN (set) DO command`

Type Internal, batch processing subcommand

Summary FOR instructs DOS to sequentially assign the variable *%%v* to each member in (*set*) and then use the variable to execute *command. v* represents any alphabetical character, and *command* represents any valid DOS command except another FOR command.

Remarks
- *%%v* can be used as a replaceable parameter in *command.*
- If FOR is entered at command level (i.e., not included in a batch file), only one % symbol should be used in the command.

Example If the command

```
FOR %%V IN (A:FILE1 B:FILE2.DOC) DO DIR %%V
```

is executed from a batch file, the result of this batch command is equivalent to entering the following two commands:

```
A>DIR FILE1
A>DIR B:FILE2.DOC
```

FORMAT (FORMAT A DISKETTE OR FIXED DISK)

Format

```
FORMAT d:[/S][/1][/8][/V][/B][/4][/N:ss]
       [/T:tt]
```

Type External

Cited Chapters 3, 8

Summary FORMAT prepares the disk in the specified drive *d* to accept information from DOS by addressing the usable area of the disk, by creating the the disk directory and the File Allocation Table (FAT), and by placing the boot record at the beginning of the disk (side 0, track 0, sector 1). FORMAT also analyzes the entire disk for any defective tracks, marking these tracks as reserved to prevent them from being allocated to a data file.

Remarks

- Please remember that when you format a disk, all information on the disk is destroyed!

- /S instructs FORMAT to copy the DOS system files (IBMBIO.COM, IBMDOS.COM, and COMMAND.COM) from the disk in the default drive to the newly formatted disk. Because IBMBIO.COM and IBMDOS.COM are hidden files, executing a DIR command on the newly formatted disk lists only COMMAND.COM. DOS marks IBMBIO.COM and IBMDOS.COM as read-only files when they are created using FORMAT /S. If you do not specify the /S parameter, no system files are copied onto the disk.

- /1 instructs FORMAT to format a 5.25 inch diskette for single-sided use. If this parameter is not specified, the disk drive type will determine the format.

- /8 instructs FORMAT to format the diskette in the specified drive (5.25 inch drives only) for 8 sectors per track. If this parameter is not specified, the FORMAT command will default to 9 or 15 sectors per track depending upon the disk drive type. Note that FORMAT always generates 9 or 15 physical sectors on each diskette track, but it tells DOS to use 8 sectors per track if you use the /8 parameter. The /V parameter cannot be used with the /8 parameter.

- /V instructs FORMAT to prompt you for a volume label after the disk has been formatted. The volume label is used for identification purposes only. The label can contain from 1 to 11 characters, using the same characters allowed for filenames. The LABEL command may be used to add or change a volume label.

- /B instructs FORMAT to format a diskette for 8 sectors per track and permanently reserve space on the diskette for the hidden system files IBMBIO.COM and IBMDOS.COM. It does not place these files on the diskette. This parameter allows you to create a diskette on which any version of DOS can be placed by using that version's SYS command. A diskette formatted without the /B option must have the hidden system files transferred to it before any other files are placed on the diskette. The /S and /V parameters cannot be used with the /B parameter.

- /4 instructs FORMAT to format a 360KB diskette in a 1.2MB diskette drive. You can format a single-sided diskette in a 1.2MB diskette drive by using both the /1 and /4 parameters.
- /N:*ss* instructs FORMAT to format *ss* sectors per track. (Valid only when used with 720KB/1.44MB and 1.2MB drives. New feature of DOS 3.30.)
- /T:*tt* instructs FORMAT to format *tt* tracks on the diskette. (Valid only when used with 720KB/1.44MB and 1.2MB drives. New feature of DOS 3.30.)
- If either /N or /T is specified, then they both must be specified. They are used to format a diskette to less than the maximum supported capacity of the diskette drive.
- FORMAT ignores any disk drive reassignments (ASSIGN).
- FORMAT should not be used with joined drives (JOIN) or substituted drives (SUBST).
- FORMAT does not work on networked drives.
- Refer to your DOS manual for a listing of which FORMAT parameters may be specified with the different disk drive types.
- Some of the parameters in the FORMAT command are used to format diskettes for different capacities. Table B.2 outlines some of these characterstics.

TABLE B.2 DISKETTE CAPACITY CHARACTERISTICS

Diskette Types	Diskette Size (Inches)	Sides	Tracks /Side	Sectors /Track	Bytes /Sector	Total Bytes	Total Bytes Available	Diskette Overhead (Bytes)
160KB	5.25	1	40	8	512	163,840	160,256	3,584
180KB	5.25	1	40	9	512	184,320	179,712	4,608
320KB	5.25	2	40	8	512	327,680	322,560	5,120
360KB	5.25	2	40	9	512	368,640	362,496	6,144
720KB	3.50	2	80	9	512	737,280	730,112	7,168
1.2MB	5.25	2	80	15	512	1,228,800	1,213,952	14,848
1.44MB	3.50	2	80	18	512	1,474,560	1,457,664	16,896

GOTO (SEQUENCE CONSTRUCT IN BATCH PROCESSING)

Format `GOTO label`

Type Internal, batch processing subcommand

Summary GOTO transfers control during the batch file execution to the line immediately after the line that begins with *:label*, where DOS continues command execution. *label* represents a string of alphanumeric (alphabetic and/or numeric) characters and is called the label name.

Remarks
- To insert a label in a batch file, you use a colon (:) followed by the label name. In fact, any line beginning with a colon (:) is interpreted as a labeled line.
- You can use more than eight characters in a label name, but only the first eight characters are significant.
- A line in a batch file beginning with a label is not displayed when the batch file executes. Thus, unreferenced labeled lines may be used to place comments in a batch file and the comments are not displayed when the file executes.

Example A batch file containing the following commands produces an indefinite sequence of REM looping ... and GOTO LOOP messages. Execution may be terminated by entering Ctrl-C (Ctrl-Break).

```
:LOOP
REM looping ...
:NOTE This message is not displayed.
GOTO LOOP
```

GRAFTABL (LOAD GRAPHICS TABLE)

Format `GRAFTABL [437 | 860 | 863 | 865 | /STATUS | ?]`

Type External

Summary GRAFTABL allows you to load into memory the character data necessary to use the extended character set in the color/graphics mode.

Remarks
- GRAFTABL has no parameters available in versions 3.xx of DOS prior to DOS 3.30.
- 437, 860, 863, and 865 are country code page numbers. Each instructs GRAFTABL to load that country's code page (complete character set) into memory. The code page identifications are 437 (United States, default), 860 (Portugal), 863 (Canada-French), and 865 (Norway and Denmark).
- /STATUS instructs GRAFTABL to display which version of the graphic character set table is in memory.

- After execution of the GRAFTABL command, ASCII characters 128 through 255 can be displayed when using the color/graphics adapter in graphics mode.
- ? instructs GRAFTABL to display a summary of its valid parameters.

GRAPHICS (SCREEN PRINT)

Format `GRAPHICS [printer][/R][/B][/LCD]`

Type External

Summary GRAPHICS allows you to print the contents of a graphics display on a printer.

Remarks
- *printer* specifies the type of printer that is attached to your computer. You should check your DOS manual for valid *printer* specifications.
- /R instructs GRAPHICS to print black and white as displayed on your screen. If /R is not specified, black is printed as white and white is printed as black.
- /B instructs GRAPHICS to print the background color.
- /LCD instructs GRAPHICS to print the screen image of an IBM PC Convertible Liquid Crystal Display. (New feature of DOS 3.30)

IF (CONDITIONAL CONSTRUCT IN BATCH PROCESSING)

Format `IF [NOT] condition command`

Type Internal, batch processing subcommand

Summary IF tests the specified *condition*. If the *condition* is true, the specified DOS *command* is executed. If the *condition* is false, the next DOS *command* in the batch file is executed. When NOT is used, it specifies that the negation or opposite of the test results is requested. Valid choices for *condition* and their interpretations are:

`EXIST filespec`	(Does *filespec* exist?)
`string1==string2`	(Are *string1* and *string2* identical?)
`ERRORLEVEL n`	(Is the exit code, returned by the preceding program, equal to or greater than *n*?)

Remarks
- Normally, the exit code of a program or DOS command is set to 0 if it completes processing successfully or to an integer greater than 0 if processing is completed unsuccessfully.

- Only the DOS commands BACKUP, FORMAT, and RESTORE set an ERRORLEVEL that can be tested. You can also set an error code in your own programs that can then be tested by the IF ERRORLEVEL subcommand.

Example Suppose a batch file contains the following lines:

```
IF EXIST MYFILE.DOC GOTO SKIP
COPY THISFILE.BAT MYFILE.DOC
:SKIP
TYPE MYFILE.DOC
```

The COPY and TYPE commands are executed if the file MYFILE.DOC does not exist in the current directory on the default drive. If the file MYFILE.DOC does exist in the current directory on the default drive, then the GOTO and TYPE commands are executed.

JOIN (JOIN DISK DRIVE TO SPECIFIC PATH NAME)

Format `JOIN [d1: {d2:\directory | /D}]`

Type External

Summary JOIN allows you to connect drive *d1* to a specified *directory* on a second drive *d2*. References to drive *d1* are now made through the specification *d2:\directory*.

Remarks
- *d2:\directory* must specify a directory one level deep from the root directory. If it exists, it must be empty. If it does not exist, JOIN creates it on drive *d2*.
- /D instructs JOIN to disconnect a join to drive *d1*.
- If no parameters are specified, JOIN displays the drives and directories that are currently joined.
- If *d1* is the default drive, it cannot be specified in the JOIN command.

KEYB (LOAD COUNTRY KEYBOARD)

Format `KEYB[keyboard-code[,[code-page][,filespec]]]`

Type External

Summary KEYB allows you to replace the standard (default) United States keyboard program with a program to support non-United States English keyboards.

Remarks
- Keyboard programs available in previous versions of DOS are not compatible with DOS 3.30.

- If you wish to replace the standard keyboard program in your computer system, you should refer to the keyboard command in your DOS manual.

LABEL (ASSIGN/CHANGE VOLUME LABEL)

Format LABEL [*d*:][*label*]

Type External

Cited Chapter 4

Summary LABEL allows you to assign, change, or remove a volume label on a disk.

Remarks

- *d* specifies the drive for the disk that you want to label.
- *label* specifies the volume label that is being assigned. *label* can contain from 1 to 11 characters, using the same characters allowed for filenames plus a space. The volume label is used for identification purposes only.
- FORMAT /V can also be used to assign a volume label to a new disk.
- If you want to check or change the volume label on a disk, enter LABEL with the appropriate drive designator and follow the prompts that are displayed by LABEL.

MKDIR [MD] (MAKE A DIRECTORY)

Format `MKDIR` *`pathspec`* or

`MD` *`pathspec`*

Type Internal

Cited Chapter 8

Summary MKDIR or MD instructs DOS to create a directory on the specified or default drive with the path given in *pathspec*.

Remarks

- Subdirectory names follow the same format rules as file names.
- The maximum length of any single path, from the root directory to its level, is 63 characters, including imbedded backslashes (\).

MODE (SET/CHANGE COMPUTER MODE)

Format Refer to your DOS manual for the multiple formats of the MODE command.

Type External

Summary The MODE command controls certain hardware-related aspects of your computer. MODE allows you to control your printer, color/graphics monitor adapter, and asynchronous communications adapter. MODE also allows you to set up and control code page switching. (New feature of DOS 3.30)

MORE (DISPLAY SCREENS OF DATA)

Format `MORE < filespec` or
`command ¦ MORE`

Type External

Cited Chapter 7

Summary MORE instructs DOS to display up to one full screen of information at a time. In the first format, MORE reads *filespec* and sends it to the standard output device (normally the display screen). In the second format, the pipe symbol (¦) causes the output from the DOS *command* to be sent (piped) to the MORE command, and MORE sends this output to the standard output device.

Remarks

- After each full screen of output, MORE pauses and displays the following message at the bottom of the screen:

  - -*More* --

  You can press any key to view the next full screen of information.

- If MORE is entered without any parameters, it echoes all lines entered back to the screen without executing them. To return to the DOS prompt, press the Ctrl-Break (Ctrl-C) key.

NLSFUNC (SUPPORT EXTENDED COUNTRY INFORMATION)

Format `NLSFUNC filespec`

Type External

Summary NLSFUNC provides support for extended country information and for code page selection in conjunction with the CHCP command.

Remarks • NLSFUNC is a new feature of DOS 3.30.

PATH (SET SEARCH DIRECTORY)

Format `PATH [;][`*`pathspec1`*` [;`*`pathspec2`*`]...]`

Type Internal

Cited Chapters 8, 9

Summary PATH instructs DOS to search *pathspec1*, *pathspec2*, ... for external commands and batch files (files having an extension of .COM, .EXE, or .BAT) that were not found while searching the current directory.

Remarks

- When PATH is entered with no parameters, it instructs DOS to display the pathspecs you specified in your last PATH command.
- Entering PATH followed by a semicolon (;) resets the extended search path to null; that is, it deletes the extended search path. This is the default condition when you boot your system.
- The PATH command searches only for executable files, that is, files having an extension of .COM, .EXE, or .BAT. The APPEND command allows you to set a search path for nonexecutable files.

PAUSE (PAUSE DURING BATCH PROCESSING)

Format PAUSE [*message*]

Type Internal, batch processing subcommand

Summary PAUSE is used in batch processing to suspend execution. If the *message* part of the command is present, it is displayed.

Remarks

- The optional *message* can be up to 121 characters long. The piping character (¦) and the I/O (Input/Output) redirection characters (< and >) cannot be used in *message*.
- You can insert the PAUSE command at strategic points in a batch file to stop the system so that you can attend to other tasks, such as changing diskettes. Pressing any key continues the execution of the batch file. Entering Ctrl-C (Ctrl-Break) terminates the batch processing.

Example The following PAUSE command will prompt you to insert the correct diskette when it is executed in a batch file:

```
PAUSE Insert the worksheet diskette in drive B.
```

PRINT (PRINT TEXT FILES)

Format PRINT [/D:*device*] [/B:*buffsize*] [/U:*busytick*]
[/M:*maxtick*] [/S:*timeslice*] [/Q:*quesize*]
[/C] [/T] [/P] [*filespec*...]

Type External

Cited Chapter 7

Summary PRINT allows you to print a text file or group of text files specified by *filespec*... while you are executing other DOS commands. PRINT also allows you to display file names in the print queue.

Remarks

- /D:*device* specifies the print *device*. If this parameter is not specified, the default device PRN is assumed. Valid values for *device* are LPT1, LPT2, LPT3, PRN, COM1, COM2, COM3, and AUX.
- /B:*buffsize* specifies the size in bytes of the print buffer. The default *buffsize* is 512 bytes.
- /Q:*quesize* specifies the maximum number of files you can have in the print queue at the same time. The default *quesize* is 10, and the range is from 1 to 32.
- /C specifies cancel mode and allows you to selectively delete (cancel) files in the print queue. The file name preceding /C and all following file names will be removed from the print queue until /P is encountered or the Enter key is pressed.
- /T specifies terminate mode and allows you to delete all files in the print queue.
- /P specifies print mode and allows you to add file names to the print queue until /C is encountered or the Enter key is pressed.
- The parameters /D, /B, /Q, /S, /U, and /M can be specified only on the first execution of the PRINT command.
- When PRINT is entered with no parameters, it instructs DOS to display the file names currently in the print queue.
- PRINT prints text files in a legible format. If you use PRINT to print another type of file (nontext file), such as a binary file, the printed information may be unreadable owing to the presence of special character codes, control characters, and escape sequences (nonprintable characters) in the file.

PROMPT (SET/RESET DOS PROMPT)

Format PROMPT [{*$param* | *string*}...]

Type Internal

Cited Chapters 8, 9

Summary PROMPT allows you to set a new DOS prompt as specified by $*param* and/or *string* or to reset the prompt to the normal DOS prompt.

Remarks • $*param* specifies particular characters to be used by PROMPT for a new DOS prompt. The dollar sign ($) is a parameter delimeter and instructs DOS to interpret the meaning of the next character (denoted by *param*) according to the following table (this table is not complete):

param	meaning
G	The > character
L	The < character
N	The default drive letter
P	The current directory path of the default drive
Q	The = character

• When PROMPT is entered with no parameters, PROMPT resets the prompt to the normal DOS prompt.

• You can freely intermix $*param* and the prompt *string* parameters on the PROMPT command line.

RECOVER (RECOVER FILES)

Format RECOVER *filespec* or
RECOVER *d*:

Type External

Summary RECOVER instructs DOS to recover a single file (denoted by *filespec*) that contains a bad sector(s), or all files on the disk in drive *d* if the disk contains a defective directory. RECOVER places the recovered files on the original disk, and marks the defective sectors so that the disk is still usable.

Remarks • If you specify *filespec*, the recovered file is given the name of the original file.

• If you specify *d*:, all files are given new names of the form FILE*nnnn*.REC where *nnnn* is the number of the file.

• If the sum of the number of files in the root directory and the number of files in each subdirectory is greater than the maximum number of file entries allowed for a root directory (112 for a 360KB diskette), multiple recovers may have to be used to save the entire disk.

Example The following command recovers the file BADFILE.DOC from the disk in drive B. The file BADFILE.DOC is read sector-by-sector, skipping bad sectors and marking them so that they will not be used.

```
A>RECOVER B:BADFILE.DOC
```

REM (DISPLAY REMARK DURING BATCH PROCESSING)

Format `REM [`*`message`*`]`

Type Internal, batch processing subcommand

Cited Chapter 9

Summary REM is used to display remarks from within an executing batch file. If *message* is specified, REM instructs DOS to display *message* when executed in a batch file.

Remarks
- If ECHO is OFF, *message* is not displayed.
- The optional *message* can be up to 123 characters long. The piping character (¦) and the I/O (Input/Output) redirection characters (< and >) cannot be used in *message*.
- The REM command helps make batch files more readable.

Example If you want to display an informative message, insert the following REM commands in your batch file:

```
REM  Processing is complete.
REM  Insert a blank diskette in drive B.
```

RENAME [REN] (RENAME FILES)

Format `RENAME` *`filespec filename`*`[.`*`ext`*`]` or
`REN` *`filespec filename`*`[.`*`ext`*`]`

Type Internal

Cited Chapter 5

Summary RENAME allows you to rename a file or group of files within the same directory. *filespec* specifies the file or files to be renamed. *filename*[*.ext*] specifies the new file name or names.

Remarks
- You can use wildcard characters to rename groups of files as long as you keep a one-to-one correspondence between the two specified parameters.

REPLACE (REPLACE FILES)

Format `REPLACE` *filespec* [*pathspec*][/A][/P][/R][/S][/W]

Type External

Summary REPLACE allows you to selectively replace files in or add files to the target directory (specified by *pathspec*) using the source file or group of files (specified by *filespec*).

Remarks

- /A instructs REPLACE to add to the target directory (*pathspec*) new files specified by *filespec* that are not in the target directory. You cannot use the parameters /A and /S together.
- /P instructs REPLACE to prompt you before adding or replacing any file in the target directory.
- /R instructs REPLACE to replace read-only files as well as unprotected files.
- /S instructs REPLACE to search all subdirectories of the target directory for files matching the source file. You cannot use the parameters /A and /S together.
- /W instructs REPLACE to wait for you to press a key before replacing or adding files.

RESTORE (RESTORE BACKUP FILES)

Format `RESTORE` *d: filespec* [/S][/P][/B:*mm-dd-yy*][/A:*mm-dd-yy*][/M][/N][/L:*time*][/E:*time*]

Type External

Cited Chapter 8

Summary RESTORE allows you to restore a file or a group of files specified by *filespec* (target) from the disk in drive *d* (source). *filespec* specifies where you want to restore the files and what files from the source disk you want to restore.

Remarks

- The files being restored must have been placed on the diskette in drive *d* (source diskette) by the BACKUP command.
- The files must be restored to the same directory and in the same order in which they were last saved by BACKUP.
- /S instructs RESTORE to restore all files in the specified directory and in its subdirectories at all levels.

- /P instructs RESTORE to prompt you before restoring files that have been changed since they were last backed up or that are marked as read-only files.
- /B, /A, /M, /N, /L, and /E are new features of DOS 3.30.
- /M instructs RESTORE to restore files that were modified or deleted since they were last backed up.
- /N instructs RESTORE to restore files that no longer exist on the target disk.
- The RESTORE command cannot be used to restore the three DOS system files IBMBIO.COM, IBMDOS.COM, and COMMAND.COM. This is a new feature of DOS 3.30. RESTORE in previous versions of DOS can be used to restore these files, but it should be used with great care.

RMDIR [RD] (REMOVE DIRECTORY)

Format `RMDIR` *`pathspec`* or
`RD` *`pathspec`*

Type Internal

Cited Chapter 8

Summary RMDIR (RD) instructs DOS to remove (delete) the directory specified by *pathspec*.

Remarks
- The directory denoted by *pathspec* must be empty before it can be removed from the disk.
- You cannot remove the current directory or the root directory.

SELECT (SELECT KEYBOARD LAYOUT, DATE, TIME)

Format `SELECT [[A: | B:] [`*`pathspec`*`]]` *`country-code keyboard-code`*

Type External

Summary SELECT allows you to install DOS on a new disk with the keyboard layout, date, and time format for a specific country. [A: | B:] specifies the source drive, and *pathspec* specifies the target drive and path where the DOS commands are to be copied.

Remarks
- SELECT uses the FORMAT and XCOPY commands and creates an AUTOEXEC.BAT file and a CONFIG.SYS file on the target disk.

SET (SET ENVIRONMENT)

Format `SET [name=[string]]`

Type Internal

Summary SET allows you to display the DOS environment strings and to insert, change, or delete environment string definitions in the DOS environment table.

Remarks

- If SET is entered with no parameter, then the current collection of environment strings is displayed.
- If *name=* is specified without *string*, then the current *name=string* is deleted from the environment.
- SET is commonly used in conjunction with batch processing.

SHARE (LOAD FILE SHARING SUPPORT)

Format `SHARE [/F:filespace][/L:locks]`

Type External

Summary SHARE allows you to support file sharing in a multiuser environment.

Remarks

- The SHARE command is used only when networking is active.
- /F:*filespace* specifies the file space in bytes that you want allocated to DOS for recording file sharing information. The default value is 2048 bytes.
- /L:*locks* specifies the number of file locks that you want. The default value is 20.

SHIFT (SHIFT BATCH PROCESSING PARAMETERS)

Format `SHIFT`

Type Internal, batch processing subcommand

Summary SHIFT allows command lines to make use of more than ten (%0 through %9) replaceable parameters.

SORT (SORT TEXT INFORMATION)

Format `SORT [/R][/+n][<filespec1][>filespec2]` or
`command ¦ SORT [/R][/+n]`

Type External

Cited Chapter 4

Summary SORT allows you to sort text information alphanumerically by its binary coded value. In the first format, SORT reads data from *filespec1* (input), sorts the data, and then sends the sorted data to *filespec2* (output). In the second format, SORT accepts input from *command*, sorts the data, and then sends the sorted data to the display unit.

Remarks

- /R instructs SORT to sort the data in reverse order.
- /+*n* instructs SORT to start the sorting processing in column *n*.
- *filespec1* specifies the input file. If it is not specified, the default is the console.
- *filespec2* specifies the output file. If it is not specified, the default is the display unit.
- *command* specifies any DOS command and its output is piped (¦) as input to SORT.

SUBST (SUBSTITUTE A CHARACTER FOR A PATHNAME)

Format `SUBST [d: {pathspec | /D}]`

Type External

Summary SUBST allows you to assign a disk drive designator (*d*:) to a specific path (*pathspec*) or to delete the assignment of a drive designator (*d*:).

Remarks

- *d*: *pathspec* instructs SUBST to assign the drive designator *d*: to *pathspec* where *d* denotes an alphabetic character and *pathspec* denotes a valid drive designator and path. Note that the character you choose for *d* depends upon the value of the LASTDRIVE configuration commmand. If you have no LASTDRIVE command in your CONFIG.SYS file, you cannot use a character greater than E for *d*.
- *d* cannot be the same as the default drive.
- *d*:/D instructs SUBST to delete the assignment of drive *d*.
- If you enter SUBST with no parameters, a list of the current substitutions will be displayed.

Example The following command assigns the designator E: to the pathspec B:\DATA\FILES:

```
A>SUBST E: B:\DATA\FILES
```

SYS (TRANSFER SYSTEM FILES)

Format `SYS d:`

Type External

Cited Chapter 3

Summary SYS instructs DOS to transfer the DOS system files IBMBIO.COM and IBMDOS.COM from the disk in the default drive to the disk in drive *d*.

Remarks

- The destination disk in drive *d* must be formatted and must have an empty directory or must have been formatted with the /S or /B parameters. (See the FORMAT command.) This is necessary because DOS startup requires that the hidden files IBMBIO.COM and IBMDOS.COM occupy the first two directory entries and because IBMBIO.COM must start at the beginning of the disk's data area.
- After the DOS system files IBMBIO.COM and IBMDOS.COM are transferred, they are marked as read-only files.
- SYS cannot be used on a network drive.

TIME (DISPLAY/SET CURRENT TIME)

Format `TIME [hh:mm:[ss[.xx]]]`

Type Internal

Cited Chapters 2, 9

Summary TIME instructs DOS to display and set the system time where *hh* specifies the hours (0 through 23), *mm* specifies minutes (0 through 59), *ss* specifies seconds (0 through 59), and *xx* specifies hundredths of a second (0 through 99).

Remarks

- If you enter TIME with no parameters, the current system time and a prompt message are displayed on the screen. At this point you may either accept the current time or enter a new time.
- The hour, minute, and second parts of the time may be separated by using a colon (:) or a period (.). A period is used to separate seconds from hundredths of a second.

- Any field in the TIME command that is not entered will be set to zero.
- When a file is created or modified, the current system date and time are recorded in the directory with the file name.
- If you have a real-time clock/calendar on your system, the TIME command in DOS 3.30 changes both the system time and the clock/calendar time. The TIME command in DOS versions previous to DOS 3.30 will not change the clock/calendar time.

TREE (DISPLAY DIRECTORY STRUCTURE)

Format `TREE [d:][/F]`

Type External

Cited Chapter 8

Summary TREE allows you to display the directory structure of the disk in drive *d* by displaying all of the directory paths that are on the disk in the specified drive. TREE also allows you to list all subdirectory and file names in the root directory and each subdirectory.

Remarks

- /F instructs TREE to list all file names that are in the root directory and each subdirectory of the disk in drive *d*.
- If *d* is not specified, the default drive is assumed.

TYPE (DISPLAY TEXT FILES)

Format `TYPE filespec`

Type Internal

Cited Chapter 7

Summary TYPE instructs DOS to display the contents of the file specified by *filespec* on the standard output device.

Remarks

- TYPE displays text files in a legible format. If you use TYPE to display another type of file (nontext file), such as a binary file, the displayed information may be unreadable owing to the presence of special character codes, control characters, and escape sequences (nondisplayable characters) in the file.

VER (DISPLAY DOS VERSION NUMBER)

Format `VER`

Type Internal

Cited Chapters 2, 9

Summary VER allows you to display your DOS version number on the standard output device.

Remarks
- The version number is of the form *X.xx*, where *X* specifies a single-digit major version number and *xx* specifies a two-digit minor revision level.

VERIFY (DISPLAY/SET DISK WRITE VERIFY STATUS)

Format `VERIFY [ON | OFF]`

Type Internal

Summary VERIFY instructs DOS to display or set the disk write-verify status.

Remarks
- When you set the disk write-verify status ON, DOS verifies that data is correctly recorded when written to a disk.
- The default status for VERIFY is OFF.
- If you enter VERIFY with no parameters, DOS displays the current status (ON or OFF) of VERIFY.

VOL (DISPLAY DISK VOLUME LABEL)

Format `VOL [d:]`

Type Internal

Cited Chapter 4

Summary VOL instructs DOS to display the volume identification label of the disk in the specified drive.

Remarks
- If drive *d* is not specified, the default drive is assumed.

XCOPY (COPY SELECTED GROUPS)

Format

```
XCOPY filespec1 [filespec2][/A]
     [/D:mm-dd-yy][/E][/M][/P][/S][/V][/W]
```

Type External

Cited Chapter 6

Summary XCOPY allows you to selectively copy files specified by *filespec1* (source) to a drive, file, or directory specified by *filespec2* (target). *filespec1* and *filespec2* may specify a drive, file, or directory path.

Remarks

- /A instructs XCOPY to copy those source files that have their archive attribute bit set to one (on). This option does not modify the archive attribute bit of the source file.
- /D:*mm-dd-yy* instructs XCOPY to copy source files that have creation or modification dates on or after the specified date, *mm-dd-yy*.
- /E instructs XCOPY to copy any subdirectory, even if it is empty. If /E is not specified, empty directories are not created. This parameter is useful when used with the /S parameter.
- /M instructs XCOPY to copy those source files that have their archive attribute bit set to one (on). This option sets off the archive attribute bit of the source file. The parameters /M and /A are incompatible.
- /P instructs XCOPY to prompt you with (Y/N)? before copying each file.
- /S instructs XCOPY to copy files in the source directory and in all subdirectories below the initial directory unless they are empty. If /S is not specified, XCOPY copies only from the specified source directory.
- /V instructs XCOPY to verify each file as it is written on the target disk.
- /W instructs XCOPY to wait before it starts copying files. This allows you to insert diskettes before XCOPY begins searching for source files.
- If no path is specified in *filespec1* (source), XCOPY begins searching for files to copy in the current directory of the source drive.
- If no file names are specified in *filespec1*, the default file name *.* is used.
- When a read-only file is copied with the XCOPY command, the read-only status is not transferred to the target file.

Appendix C: Preparing a DOS 3.30 System Diskette

The DOS Version 3.30 package contains two 360KB diskettes, the DOS Startup diskette and the DOS Operating diskette. The DOS Startup diskette must be used to boot your system. It also contains some external DOS commands that are used to initially set up your system. The DOS Operating diskette contains the remaining external DOS commands, but it cannot be used to boot your system. A single 360KB diskette does not have enough room to hold the DOS system files IBMBIO.COM, IBMDOS.COM, and COMMAND.COM along with all of the external DOS 3.30 commands (programs). The steps given below show you how to create a bootable diskette that does contain most of the external DOS 3.30 commands. This diskette will be referred to as your DOS System diskette. Before you work through the steps given below, you should make backup copies of your DOS Startup diskette and your DOS Operating diskette. This can be accomplished by following the steps outlined in Chapter 2 and by noting that the DISKCOPY command (program) is on the DOS Operating diskette.

MAKING A DOS 3.30 SYSTEM DISKETTE USING TWO DISKETTE DRIVES

1. Insert the DOS Startup diskette in drive A.
2. Insert a blank (target) diskette in drive B.
3. Boot the system if it is not already booted.

4. With A> as the prompt, enter the following DOS command:

```
A>FORMAT B:/S
```

5. Press Enter after the first prompt message.
6. Enter N after the second prompt message.
7. With A> as the prompt, enter each of the following DOS commands:

```
A>COPY FASTOPEN.EXE B:
A>COPY FDISK.COM B:
A>COPY REPLACE.EXE B:
A>COPY SYS.COM B:
```

8. Remove the DOS Startup diskette from drive A.
9. Insert the DOS Operating diskette in drive A.
10. With A> as the prompt, enter the following DOS command:

```
A>COPY *.COM B:
```

    Twenty files are copied from the DOS Operating diskette to the target diskette in drive B.
11. With A> as the prompt, enter each of the following DOS commands:

```
A>DEL B:BASIC*.COM
A>DEL B:DEBUG.COM
A>DEL B:RESTORE.COM
A>COPY *.EXE B:
```

    Four .COM files are deleted from the target diskette, and eight .EXE files are copied to the target diskette.
12. Remove the DOS Operating diskette from drive A and store it and the DOS Startup diskette in a safe place.
13. Remove the target diskette from drive B and label it
    `IBM PC-DOS, Version 3.30, System` or
    `MS-DOS, Version 3.30, System`
    This diskette is your DOS System diskette.

Note: KEYB, MODE, NLSFUNC, RESTORE, and SELECT are the only DOS 3.30 commands that are not on your newly prepared DOS 3.30 System diskette.

Index